Rodgers & Hammerstein's
The King and I

Music by
Richard Rodgers

Book & Lyrics by
Oscar Hammerstein II

Based on "Anna and the King of Siam" by

Margaret Landon

Original Choreography by Jerome Robbins

Orchestrations by
Robert Russel Bennett

Dance & Incidental Music Arranged by Trude Rittman

CONCORD
THEATRICALS

ISBN 978-0-573-70927-2

www.concordtheatricals.com
www.concordtheatricals.co.uk

This work is published by R&H Theatricals, an imprint of Concord Theatricals Corp.

MUSIC AND THIRD-PARTY MATERIALS USE NOTE

IMPORTANT BILLING AND CREDIT REQUIREMENTS

THE KING AND I was Presented by the Messrs. Rodgers & Hammerstein, production company in St. James Theatre, New York on March 29, 1951. The performance was directed by John van Druten, choreography by Jerome Robbins, settings and lighting by Jo Mielziner, costumes by Irene Sharaff, musical direction by Frederick Dvonch, orchestrations by Robert Russell Bennett, dance and incidental music arranged by Trude Rittmann. The cast was as follows:

CAPTAIN ORTON . . . . Charles Francis

LOUIS LEONOWENS . . . . Sandy Kennedy

ANNA LEONOWENS . . . . Gertrude Lawrence

THE INTERPRETER . . . . Leonard Graves

THE KRALAHOME . . . . John Juliano

THE KING . . . . Yul Brynner

PHRA ALACK . . . . Len Mence

TUPTIM . . . . Doretta Morrow

LADY THIANG . . . . Dorothy Sarnoff

PRINCE CHULALONGKORN . . . . Johnny Stewart

PRINCESS YING YAOWALAK . . . . Baayork Lee

LUN THA . . . . Larry Douglas

SIR EDWARD RAMSEY . . . . Robin Craven

PRINCESSES AND PRINCES . . . . Crisanta Cornejo,
Andrea Del Rosario, Marcia James,
Barbara Luna, Nora Baez, Corrine St. Denis,
Bunny Warner, Rodolfo Cornejo, Robert Cortazal,
Thomas Griffin, Alfonso Maribo,
James Maribo, Orlando Rodigeuz

THE ROYAL DANCERS . . . . Jamie Bauer, Lee Becker,
Marry Burr, Gemze DeLappe, Shellie Farrell,
Marilyn Gennaro, Evelyn Giles, Ina Kurland,
Nancy Lynch, Michiko, Helen Murielle,
Prue Ward, Dusty Worrall, Yuriko

WIVES . . . . Stephanie Augustine, Marcia James,
Ruth Korda, Suzanne Lake, Gloria Marlowe,
Carolyn Maye, Helen Merritt, Phillis Wilcox

AMAZONS . . . . Geraldine Hamburg, Maribel Hammer,
Norma Larkin, Miriam Lawrence

PRIESTS . . . . Duane Camp, Joseph Caruso,
Leonard Graves, Jack Matthew, Ed Preston

SLAVES AND MUSICIANS . . . . Doria Avila, Raul Celada,
Beau Cunningham, Tommy Gomez

ORIGINAL PRODUCTION

Tryout:
Shubert Theatre, New Haven
February 26 – March 3, 1951
Shubert Theatre, Boston
March 5 – 24, 1951
New York Run:
St. James Theatre
March 29, 1951 – March 20, 1954
1,246 Performances

CHARACTERS

CAPTAIN ORTON – A British sea captain

LOUIS LEONOWENS – Anna's Son

ANNA LEONOWENS – A British schoolteacher, traveling to Siam, engaged to teach the Royal Children

THE INTERPRETER – The King's interpreter

THE KRALAHOME – The King's Executive Officer

THE KING – The King of Siam (based on the historical King Mongkut)

PHRA ALACK – Secretary and chief footman to the King

LUN THA – A Burmese scholar and envoy

TUPTIM – A Burmese slave

LADY THIANG – The King's head wife – mother of Prince Chulalongkorn

PRINCE CHULALONGKORN – The King's eldest son and heir

SIR EDWARD RAMSAY – A British diplomat

PRINCESS YING YAOWALAK – One of the youngest of the King's daughters

NINE PRINCES AND EIGHT PRINCESSES – The King's children

EIGHTEEN ROYAL DANCERS (SKILLED ENOUGH TO EXECUTE "THE SMALL HOUSE OF UNCLE THOMAS" BALLET)

TEN PRIESTS OF SIAM

TEN ROYAL WIVES – The King's wives

FEMALE GUARDS (AMAZONS) – Guards of the Royal Wives

ENSEMBLE: Large singing and dancing ensemble consisting of Royal Dancers, Wives, Priests, Guards and the children of the King.

SETTING

The action of the play takes place in and around the King's Palace, Bangkok, Siam during the early 1860s.

CASTING NOTE

The King and I is inspired by the novel *Anna and the King of Siam* by Margaret Landon and is based on the lives of real people. The story takes place in Siam during the early 1860s in and around the Royal Palace. Many of the characters are Siamese or from surrounding countries and of Asian heritage. The actors should be cast accordingly. The use of make-up or prosthetics to alter an actor's ethnicity is prohibited.

NOTES ON THE ORIGINAL BROADWAY PRODUCTION

These notes were culled from conversations with Gemze de Lappe, a performer in both the original Broadway cast and the 1956 20th Century Fox film version of *The King and I*. Ms. de Lappe also assisted Jerome Robbins in mounting subsequent productions of *The King and I*, including the original West End production in London in 1953.

CHARACTERS

THE KING

The character of the King is that of a man who is secure in his power. He is serious and intellectual and anxious to bring Western knowledge to Siam. He is not a man of anger or petulance. Because he has never known anything but absolute and unquestioned authority there is little reason for him to need to resort to bombastic behavior. This changes only as Anna begins to challenge him and he is forced to pit his vision of a civilized Siam against his own ego. When the King is first revealed (in Act One, Scene Three) the mood surrounding him is one of serenity and decorum. The court dancers and music should provide an effect akin to classical music being played softly in the background. He sits on a dais, which places him physically and spiritually above everyone else in the room. His subjects do not look directly at him. In his presence their hands are kept in praying position. The court's behavior in front of the King is always one of utmost respect.

ANNA

Anna is in many ways a very modern woman. To her, business is business. She is confident, she understands the job she has been hired to do, and is she is willing to stand up for what she believes is correct. Her flaw is her temperament. Without this flaw she could be mistakenly perceived as merely a colonialist, which misses the point of the story.

LOUIS

Louis is about eight. He has been brought up in the middle class of the Victorian era. He is polite to and respectful of those around him, but sincerely so. He should appear to be a couple of years younger than Chulalongkorn.

CHULALONGKORN

Chulalongkorn is about ten. He looks to be a couple of years older than Louis. As the Crown Prince he is given deferential treatment by the entire court. Only his father outranks him. His manner can seem rigid and his bearing militaristic as he tries to walk in his father's footsteps, on his way to becoming the king his parents and his country need him to be.

TUPTIM

Tuptim should not show herself as a victim at the start of the play *("My Lord and Master")*. She becomes a victim as the play progresses. She arrives at the Siamese court not only angry and indignant at being made a gift but consternated that she is not allowed to communicate with Lun Tha, her lover. Eventually her love for Lun Tha gets the best of her, and she reveals herself to disastrous results for both of them.

AMAZONS

These women guards should be in every scene in which the Wives appear. They are strong, strapping women whose demeanor tells us they are willing and able to protect the Wives, who have been placed in their care.

ATTITUDES & FACES

The Royal Dancers in the Ballet do not look up or out, but keep their eyes averted down. The exception is the expression of fear which is accompanied by an exaggerated opening of the eyes.

BASIC VOCABULARY OF THE BOWS

Throughout the play the members of the court perform different kinds of ceremonial bows to the King and to each other. These are specified as:

[A] Prostrate (Kneeling, sitting on heels, body bent forward with forearms, palms and forehead on the floor)

[B] On One Knee

[C] Standing (Hands in prayer position, bending from the upper back)

[D] Kneeling (Sitting on heels)

[E] Kneeling High (Straight from the knees up)

When leaving the presence of the King all member of his court back away from him respectfully, leaning forward with hands in prayer position. At a certain point they may turn and exit the stage quickly.

These bows are demonstrated in the choreographic video.

CHOREOGRAPHIC NOTES

#6. Vignettes and Dance

In the original production the dancers being made up in the corridor were not the same dancers who were preset in the King's library and were dancing for him as he was revealed in Act One, Scene Three.

The dance being performed for the King should set a mood of dignity and intellectual sophistication. The mood of the musical underscore and the dancing should be one of soft murmurs – beautiful, gentle, lovely movement, slightly sensuous and serene.

This dance is demonstrated in the choreographic video.

#11. The March of Siamese Children

This is the introduction of the King's Children, who enter from upstage right, one by one, bow before the King, cross down to Anna, and touch her hands to their foreheads. They then back up to take kneeling positions stage right, having been guided into place by their mothers.

1st CHILD (**GIRL**) holding a doll in her arms, is carried on by one of the Amazons, who sets her down at the bottom of the steps. She gives the doll to the Amazon before bowing to the King. She then goes to Anna and is guided back into position by her mother. The Amazon backs off right.

2nd CHILD (**BOY**) is carried on by an Amazon, bows to the King, goes to Anna and is then guided back into position by his mother. The Amazon exits right.

3rd and 4th CHILDREN (**TWINS**) walk on together holding hands, do their bows together and are guided back into position by their mother.

5th CHILD (**BOY**) walks on, does bow to King, is about to touch Anna's hands, looks at his own hands, realizes they are dirty, rubs his hands on the seat of his trousers, then does his bow to Anna and is guided back into position by his mother.

6th CHILD (**GIRL**) walks on, stares at Anna all through her bow to the King, fascinated, then crosses down to Anna, does a normal bow to her, then makes a grab at Anna's skirt, lifting it and looking beneath it. The

Kings steps forward, angrily claps his hands, and she is shamefacedly guided back into position by her mother.

7th CHILD (**PRINCE CHULALONGKORN**) At bar 53 of the music Chulalongkorn strides on proudly, stopping at center and facing front on the 13th beat (the downbeat of bar 59). On the 1st beat of bar 61 he comes down center, turning on the 5th beat (downbeat of bar 62) to face his father on the 9th beat (downbeat of bar 65). On the 13th beat (downbeat of bar 67) he drops to his knees. On the 15th beat (downbeat of bar 68) he prostrates himself to his father. On the 1st beat of the next bar (downbeat of bar 69) he straightens up. On the 3rd beat (downbeat of bar 70) he stands. On the 5th beat (downbeat of bar 71) the King returns his bow. On the 9th beat (downbeat of bar 73) Chulalongkorn moves to Anna. They regard each other, and at bar 77 she slowly curtseys to him, deeply and respectfully. At bar 79 he responds with the same bow he exchanged with his father. At bar 81 he backs up and is received by Lady Thiang, who guides him to his place as the next child enters (bar 83). All of Chulalonghorn's moves should be made with military precision and bespeak his regal bearing. He is his father's son.

8th CHILD (**BOY**) performs a straightforward bow to the King and a curtsey to Mrs. Anna.

9th CHILD (**GIRL**) After her bows to the King and Anna she turns and starts to walk into position right. Her mother points to her and indicates that she has forgotten something and that she should turn back. Realizing her mistake, she turns to Anna, takes a red rose from the hair and offers it to Anna. Then she backs into position assisted by her mother.

10th CHILD (**PRINCESS YING YAOWLAK**) enters smiling and starts to mount the dais to embrace her father. He hastily pushes her away, she bows. Going to Anna she is crestfallen, but as she retreats from Anna the King smiles at her and she smiles back at him joyously.

11th CHILD (**BOY**) performs a straightforward bow to the King and a curtsey to Mrs. Anna.

12th CHILD (**SMALLEST BOY**) is carried on by an Amazon, who sets him down and exits right. The child crosses to the King, who is looking in another direction, and tugs at his penuang. Receiving the King's attention he bows and then bows to Anna and backs into position.

On the final beat of music all Wives and Children prostrate themselves to the King and Anna.

#31. *"Western People Funny"*

The staging needs to be simple and believable. The comedy derives from the Wives reaction to wearing Western clothing and especially Western shoes for the first time. Western clothes are very restrictive to these women. They can't move in them the way they are used to moving in their own clothes. They find themselves, some with one shoe off and one shoe on, having trouble sitting down and maneuvering past each other. If the actors believe in the situation the audience will accept it. The joke as Hammerstein has written it is not on the Siamese but on the Westerners who sentimentalize them. (*"They think they civilize us whenever they advise us to learn to make the same mistake that they are making too".*)

#38. *"The Small House of Uncle Thomas"* (Ballet)

The dancers never look directly out at the audience, as they would always avert their eyes from the King.

One of the small children (but not the smallest) should portray Buddha.

The bows that the six principals take at the end of the ballet are demonstrated in the choreographic video.

[NOTE: Gemze de Lappe (the original King Simon of Legree) points out that during the rehearsals of the original production she watched Yul Brynner to help her create her own King character. Since the ballet is Tuptim's invention she has created the character of King Simon of Legree with her anger toward the King of Siam in mind.]

#49. *EXIT MUSIC (Bows at end of Show)*

Corps Dancers and Singers

Children

Supporting Roles (Sir Edward, Phra Alak, Captain Orton)

Solo Dancers

Principal Roles

ENCORES

Although the encores for both *"Hello, Young Lovers"* and *"Getting To Know You"* have been retained in the piano vocal score and instrumental parts, this has been done for historical purposes only. Encores were often called for in an era when it was not unusual for a star of Gertrude Lawrence's magnitude to provide them. This was especially the case as the songs were being introduced for the first time. However, keeping in mind that the running time of the original Broadway production was three hours and two minutes, these encores should not be included in contemporary productions of *The King and I* unless the audience demands them.

MUSICAL SYNOPSIS

ACT I

["OVERTURE"]
Scene One: Deck of the Chow Phya
["I WHISTLE A HAPPY TUNE"] .... Anna and Louis

Scene Two: A Palace Corridor
["VIGNETTES AND DANCE"] .... Court Dances

Scene Three: The King's Library in the Royal Palace
["MY LORD AND MASTER"] .... Tuptim
["THERE IS A HAPPY LAND"] .... Lady Thiang
["HELLO, YOUNG LOVERS"]................................Anna
["THE MARCH OF
        SIAMESE CHILDREN"] .... Royal Siamese Children

Scene Four: The Palace Grounds
["BE IT EVER SO HUMBLE"] – Scene Before Curtain............Children
["A PUZZLEMENT"] .... King

Scene Five: The Schoolroom
["SCHOOLROOM SCENE"].....................Children and Wives
["GETTING TO KNOW YOU"] .... Anna, Children and Wives
["WE KISS IN A SHADOW"]....................Lun Tha and Tuptim

Scene Six: A Palace Corridor
["A PUZZLEMENT"] – Reprise...............Chulalongkorn and Louis

Scene Seven: Anna's Bedroom
["SHALL I TELL YOU WHAT I THINK OF YOU?"]................Anna
["SOMETHING WONDERFUL"] .... Lady Thiang

Scene Eight: A Palace Corridor
["SOMETHING WONDERFUL"] – Reprise .... Lady Thiang

Scene Nine: The King's Library
["FINALE ACT I"] .... King and Company

ACT II

ACT I

Scene One: Deck of The Chow Phya

MUSIC 1: ["OVERTURE"]

(Deck of the Chow Phya, a ship that has sailed from Singapore, up the Gulf of Siam, and is now making its way slowly along the winding river that approaches Bangkok. The year is 1862. On the deck are several boxes and crates of furniture suggesting Victorian household effects crated in the Orient with bamboo, rattan cloth, woven slats, etc. A step unit stage left (dockside) leads to the gangway.)

MUSIC 2: ["OPENING ACT ONE (ARRIVAL AT BANGKOK)"]

(AT RISE: [measure 11] **CAPTAIN ORTON,** *a middle-aged Englishman, is leaning on the binnacle – a housing for a ship's compass – smoking a pipe. As soon as the curtain is up* **LOUIS** *runs on.)*

ORTON. Hello, Laddy.

LOUIS. *(Entering, then mounting the steps of the gangway to look out on the river.)* How near are we to Bangkok, Captain?

ORTON. *(Indicating out over the audience.)* See that cluster of lights jutting out into the river? That's it. That's Bangkok.

LOUIS. *(Seeing the crates and boxes.)* Oh, look! All our boxes!

ORTON. Aye, and a fair lot they are.

LOUIS. We packed everything we had in our Singapore house – furniture and everything.

ANNA. *(Offstage.)* Louis! Where are you?

LOUIS. Here I am, mother.

*(**ANNA** enters. The music fades out.)*

ANNA. Oh! There you are.

LOUIS. *(Running to meet her as she enters.)* Mother! Mother, Look! There's Bangkok! Do you see, Mother? That cluster of lights that stick out into the river. That's Bangkok!

ANNA. *(Laughing.)* I see, Louis, I see them. It's exciting, isn't it?

LOUIS. Will the King of Siam come down to the dock to meet us?

ANNA. The King himself? I don't think so. Kings don't as a rule.

ORTON. *(With earnest concern.)* I wonder if you know what you're facing, Ma'am – an Englishwoman here in the East.

LOUIS. *(Running down right, looking out toward the audience, and pointing over the imaginary rail.)* Look, mother! Look at that boat!

*(**ANNA** and **ORTON** look out over the audience, following **LOUIS'** eyes. Two native deck hands enter from right, carrying a*

small Victorain trunk with a domed top and handles on each end. They place the trunk right center and exit.)

Look at the dragon's head in the bow, and all the men standing up, carrying torches.

ORTON. That's the Royal barge!

LOUIS. Do you suppose that's the King, the man sitting under the gold canopy?

ORTON. That's the Kralohome.

(Explaining to ANNA.)

Sort of "Prime Minister" – the King's right hand man, you might say.

ANNA. Do you suppose he's coming out to meet us?

ORTON. No doubt of it. They'll wait until we pass them. Then they'll come around our stern.

(He starts to go, then turns back.)

Ma'am...if I might be allowed to offer you a word of warning...

ANNA. What is it, Captain?

ORTON. *(Indicating the barge.)* That man has power, and he can use it *for* you or *against* you.

ANNA. Oh, Captain, I don't...

ORTON. I'm just telling you, Ma'am. I think you should know.

MUSIC 3: ["I WHISTLE A HAPPY TUNE"]

(A sound comes from the river, the a cappella chant of oarsmen marking the cadence of their stroke.)

MEN. *(Off-stage.)*
OH—
OH—

> *(This chant continues under the following scene and segues as one into the vamp [measure 7] which begins the song.)*

ANNA. Thank you, Captain.

> **(CAPTAIN ORTON** *exits.)*

LOUIS. Look, mother! They're closer!

> *(With amazement, as he gets a better view, still looking out front over the imaginary rail.)*

Mother! The Prime Minister is *naked*!

ANNA. *(Crosses down to* **LOUIS.***)* Hush, Louis. That's not a nice word. He's not naked.

> *(She looks again.)*

Well, he's *half* naked.

LOUIS. They all look rather horrible, don't they, mother?

> *(He draws a little closer to her and takes her hand.)*

Father would not have liked us to be afraid, would he?

ANNA. *(Looks at him.)* No, Louis. Father would not have liked us to be afraid.

LOUIS. Mother, does anything ever frighten you?

ANNA. Sometimes.

LOUIS. What do you do?

ANNA. *(Confession.)* I whistle.

LOUIS. Oh, that's why you whistle.

> *(The chanting of the oarsmen is now picked up by a musical vamp [measure 7] in the orchestra.)*

ANNA. *(Laughing.)* Yes, Louis. That's why I whistle.

> *(She sings.)*

WHENEVER I FEEL AFRAID
I HOLD MY HEAD ERECT
AND WHISTLE A HAPPY TUNE,
SO NO ONE WILL SUSPECT
          I'M AFRAID.
WHILE SHIVERING IN MY SHOES
I STRIKE A CARELESS POSE

> *(She strikes a pose.)*

AND WHISTLE A HAPPY TUNE,
AND NO ONE EVER KNOWS
          I'M AFRAID.

> *(**LOUIS** backs upstage and sits on the left side of the Victorian trunk. **ANNA** follows him.)*

THE RESULT OF THIS DECEPTION
IS VERY STRANGE TO TELL,
FOR WHEN I FOOL THE PEOPLE I FEAR
I FOOL MYSELF AS WELL!

> *(**ANNA** sits on trunk to the right of **LOUIS**.)*

I WHISTLE A HAPPY TUNE,
AND EV'RY SINGLE TIME
THE HAPPINESS IN THE TUNE
CONVINCES ME THAT I'M
          NOT AFRAID.
MAKE BELIEVE YOU'RE BRAVE,
AND THE TRICK WILL TAKE YOU FAR.
YOU MAY BE AS BRAVE

AS YOU MAKE BELIEVE YOU ARE.

> (**ANNA** *whistles a strain of the melody.*)

YOU MAY BE AS BRAVE
AS YOU MAKE BELIEVE YOU ARE.

> (**ANNA** *embraces* **LOUIS** *as the music ends. On the applause the music begins again.* **LOUIS** *speaks over the music.*)

LOUIS. *(After a moment's reflection.)* I think that's a very good idea, mother. A *very* good idea.

ANNA. It *is* a good idea, isn't it?

LOUIS. *(Rising and crossing center.)* You know, I don't think I shall ever be afraid again.

ANNA. Good!

> (**LOUIS** *nods and resumes singing the refrain.*)

LOUIS.
WHILE SHIVERING IN MY SHOES
I STRIKE A CARELESS POSE

> (*He does an imitation of* **ANNA***'s pose.*)

AND WHISTLE A HAPPY TUNE,
AND NO ONE EVER KNOWS
                    I'M AFRAID.

> (**ANNA** *rises and joins in.*)

BOTH.
THE RESULT OF THIS DECEPTION
IS VERY STRANGE TO TELL,
FOR WHEN I FOOL THE PEOPLE I FEAR
I FOOL MYSELF AS WELL!
I WHISTLE A HAPPY TUNE,
AND EV'RY SINGLE TIME

THE HAPPINESS IN THE TUNE
CONVINCES ME THAT I'M
                NOT AFRAID.

(They do not see four **SIAMESE GUARDS,** *naked from the waist up, with knives in their belts, come over the rail, down the gangway, and stand two on either side of the gangway, arms akimbo.)*

MAKE BELIEVE YOU'RE BRAVE,
AND THE TRICK WILL TAKE YOU FAR.
YOU MAY BE AS BRAVE
AS YOU MAKE BELIEVE YOU ARE –

(On this last word **ANNA** *turns, sees the formidable-looking* **SIAMESE GUARDS,** *and gasps in terror.* **LOUIS** *sees them, too, and clutches his mother's arm.* **ANNA** *resumes whistling, alone [measure 115]. She urges* **LOUIS** *to whistle too. He joins her. They are more frightened than they would like anyone to know.* **ORTON** *enters and interupts them while they are still whistling [measure 120].)*

ORTON.   *(Coming on hurriedly, followed by two Deckhands.)* Clear that away!

(The Deckhands remove the trunk.)

Ma'am, I wouldn't whistle.

(The whistling stops.)

The Kralahome might think it disrespectful.

(The music fades out.)

ANNA. Oh, was I whistling! Sorry, I didn't realize.

(The **INTERPRETER** *comes over the rail and down the steps.)*

INTERPRETER. *(Rather insolently, to* ANNA.*)* Good evening, Sir. Welcome to Siam.

> *(He turns his back on her and prostrates himself, as do the four* SIAMESE GUARDS.*)*

LOUIS. He called you sir!

ANNA. Hush, dear, hush!

> *(The* KRALAHOME *comes over the rail slowly and with terrifying majesty. He is naked from the waist up, except for several necklaces.)*

MUSIC 4: ["INCIDENTAL FOR DIALOGUE"]

> *(The* INTERPRETER *sits up as the* KRALAHOME *addresses him in Siamese. This is pantomimed to the musical cue [measure 1].)*

> *(At this point, and throughout the play, the Siamese language will be represented by certain sounds made in the orchestra. Siamese words will never be literally pronounced. Music, accompanied by hand gestures, will symbolize them.)*

INTERPRETER. *(Crawling to* ANNA *and relaying the* KRALAHOME's *questions.)* Sir, His Excellency wishes to know – are you lady who will be schoolmistress of royal children?

ANNA. Yes.

INTERPRETER. Have you friends in Bangkok?

ANNA. I know no one in Bangkok at all.

> *(Crawling back to the* KRALAHOME *the* INTERPRETER *pantomimes this [measure 4]. The* KRALAHOME *pamtomimes further questions to the* INTERPRETER *[measure 7].)*

INTERPRETER. Are you married, sir?

ANNA. I am a widow.

INTERPRETER. What manner of man – your deceased husband?

ANNA. My husband was an officer in Her Majesty's Army in...

> *(She suddenly stiffens.)*

Tell your master his business with me is in my capacity of schoolteacher to the Royal children. He has no right to pry into my personal affairs.

> **(ORTON** *tries to signal a warning, but she turns to him impatiently.)*

ORTON. I don't think I would, Ma'am...

ANNA. *(Interupting him.)* Well, he hasn't, Captain Orton.

> *(The* **INTERPRETER** *pantomimes her message to the* **KRALAHOME** *[measure 9]. The* **KRALAHOME** *gives the* **INTERPRETER** *a kick on the shoulder [measure 12] which sends him sprawling out of the way.)*

LOUIS. *(To* ANNA, *pointing toward the* KRALAHOME.*)* I don't like that man!

KRALAHOME. In foreign country is best you like everyone – until you leave.

ANNA. *(Startled.)* Your Excellency. I had no idea you spoke English.

KRALAHOME. It is not necessary for you to know everything at once. You come with me now. Your boxes are carried to Palace – later.

ANNA. No. Not to the Palace. I am not living at the Palace.

KRALAHOME. Who say?

ANNA. The King say... Says! The King has promised me twenty pounds a month and a house of my own.

KRALAHOME. King do not always remember what he promise. If I tell him he break his promise, I will make anger in him. I think it is better I make anger in him about larger matters.

ANNA. But all I want is ten minutes' audience with him.

KRALAHOME. King very busy now. New Year's celebrations just finishing. Fireworks every night. Cremation of late Queen just starting.

ANNA. Oh. You have lost your Queen. I am so sorry. When did she die?

KRALAHOME. Four years ago... With cremation ceremony comes also fireworks.

ANNA. And what am I to do in the meantime?

KRALAHOME. In the meantime you wait – in Palace.

ANNA. *(Firmly.)* Your Excellency, I will teach in the Palace, but I must have a house of my own – where I can go at the end of the day when my duties are over.

KRALAHOME. What you wish to do in evening that cannot be done in Palace?

ANNA. How dare you!

(Controlling herself.)

I'm sorry Your Excellency, but you don't understand. I came here to work. I must support myself and my young son. And I shall take nothing less than what I have been promised.

KRALAHOME. You will tell King this?

ANNA. I will tell King this.

(The faint suggestion of a smile curls the corner of the KRALAHOME's mouth.)

KRALAHOME. It will be very interesting meeting. You come now?

(ANNA does not answer.)

You come now, or you can stay on boat. I do not care!

(He turns toward gangway and starts to go.)

ORTON. *(Going to ANNA, sympathetically.)* Ma'am, if you wish to stay on my ship and return to Singapore...

ANNA. No, thank you, Captain Orton.

(To KRALAHOME.)

Your Excellency – I will go with you. I have made a bargain, and I shall live up to my part of it. But I expect a bargain to be kept on both sides. I shall go with you, Your Excellency.

KRALAHOME. To the Palace?

ANNA. *(Grimly.)* For the time being.

MUSIC 5: ["EXIT (I WHISTLE A HAPPY TUNE)"]

(The KRALAHOME smiles and exits over the ship's rail. ANNA turns to ORTON.)

Goodbye, Captain Orton, and thank you very much for everything.

(Turning to LOUIS, prompting him.)

Louis!

LOUIS. *(Shaking hands.)* Goodbye, Captain.

(ANNA and LOUIS begin to exit.)

ORTON. Good-bye, laddy.

> *(As they turn from the captain,* **ANNA** *and* **LOUIS** *are confronted by the* **INTERPRETER** *and the* **SIAMESE GUARDS** *standing in a line, their arms folded, their faces stern.* **ANNA** *and* **LOUIS** *pause, then raise their chins and whistle "a happy tune" as they walk by the men and start to climb the gangway. The music rises as the scene ends.)*

Scene Two: A Palace Corridor

(A Palace corridor [in one], several weeks later.)

MUSIC 6: ["VIGNETTES AND DANCE"]

(AT RISE: Several Court Dancers are being prepared to dance for the **KING**. *Some of the dancers are having their costumes adjusted by attendants, and some are having last-minute touches added to their faces by make-up experts. Excitement, haste and anxiety pervade the scene. At measure 83 an attendant enters and claps his hands quickly five times, summoning the dancers to the* **KING***'s presence. The dancers bustle off promptly, their attendants making their exit on the opposite side. At measure 94 the corridor drop rises to reveal the* **KING***'s library.)*

Scene Three: The King's Library In The Royal Palace

(Immediately following. The room is a large study, lined with books. The dressing of the bookcases is not specific but should should show the wide range of the KING's *interests. There is a globe stage right, mounted on a stand and within concentric circles. There is also a microscope and a table-top model of a steam locomotive. Up left of center is a dais, which serves as the* KING's *throne. Behind all of this are two low steps ascending to a hallway that runs across the back of the entire set. This hallway leads to other rooms in the Palace. Beyond it is a terrace and, beyond the terrace, a skyline framed with exotic trees and temples.)*

(AT RISE: [measure 98] The KING *is seated cross-legged on the dais, reading his mail as* PHRA ALACK, *his secretary waits nearby. The* KING *pays only scant attention to the dancers, who have now assembled and are dancing languorously stage right. Their dance reflects the serenity of the* KING's *surroundings. At length he throws the last letter at the secretary [measure 113], rises and snaps his fingers [measure 114], dismissing* PHRA ALACK *and the dancers, who retire quickly. The* KING *beckons to someone offstage [measure 115]. The* KRALAHOME *enters.)*

KING. Well, well, well?

KRALAHOME. I have been meaning to speak to you about English schoolteacher. She is waiting to see you.

KING. She is in Siam? How long?

KRALAHOME. Two weeks, three weeks. She has needed disciplining, Your Majesty. She objects to living in Palace. Talks about house she say you promise her.

KING. I do not recollect such promise. Tell her I will see her. I will see her in a moment.

> (*Over the* **KRALAHOME**'s *shoulder, the* **KING** *sees* **LUN THA** *enter, preceded by a female palace attendant.*)

Who? Who? Who?

KRALAHOME. Your Majesty, this is Lun Tha, emissary from court of Burma.

KING. Ah! You are here for copying of famous Bangkok temple.

> (*To* **KRALAHOME**.)

I have give permission.

KRALAHOME. (*As* **TUPTIM** *is carried on a palanquin, by four Amazons.*) He bring you present from Prince of Burma.

KING. Am I to trust a ruler of Burma? Am I to trust this present they send me, or is she a spy?

TUPTIM. (*Stepping off the palanquin, which is then carried off by the Amazons.*) I am not a spy... My name is Tuptim. You are pleased that I speak English? My name is Tuptim.

> (*The* **KING** *crosses to the* **KRALAHOME**, *looking at* **TUPTIM** *appraisingly, then nods to the* **KRALAHOME**, *who signals* **TUPTIM** *to turn around. She does so and drops to her knees. The* **KING** *walks around her slowly, darts a brief, enigmatic look at the* **KRALAHOME** *and walks off.*)

KRALAHOME. King is pleased with you. He likes you.

(He dismisses **LUN THA** *and leaves. Before going out,* **LUN THA** *exchanges a worried, helpless look with* **TUPTIM. TUPTIM,** *rising, turns and looks toward where the* **KING** *made his exit, bitterness and hatred in her eyes.)*

MUSIC 7: ["MY LORD AND MASTER"]

TUPTIM. The King is pleased!

(She sings.)

HE IS PLEASED WITH ME,
MY LORD AND MASTER
DECLARES HE'S PLEASED WITH ME,
WHAT DOES HE MEAN?

WHAT DOES HE KNOW OF ME,
THIS LORD AND MASTER?
WHEN HE HAS LOOKED AT ME
WHAT HAS HE SEEN?

SOMETHING YOUNG,
SOFT AND SLIM,
PAINTED CHEEK,
TAP'RING LIMB,

SMILING LIPS
ALL FOR HIM,
EYES THAT SHINE
JUST FOR HIM.
SO HE THINKS,
JUST FOR HIM!

THOUGH THE MAN MAY BE
MY LORD AND MASTER,
THOUGH HE MAY STUDY ME
AS HARD AS HE CAN,
THE SMILE BENEATH MY SMILE
HE'LL NEVER SEE,

HE'LL NEVER KNOW
I LOVE ANOTHER MAN.
HE'LL NEVER KNOW
I LOVE ANOTHER MAN!

>*(The* **KING** *enters and mounts the dais.* **TUPTIM** *immediately resumes her humble and obediant attitude.)*

(Hands together, bowing.) Your Majesty wishes me to leave?

KING. I will tell you when I wish you to leave.

>*(***TUPTIM** *retires upstage and kneels, sitting on her heels.)*

KRALAHOME. *(Entering, ushering in* **ANNA***, who is followed by two Amazons.)* Madame Leonowens.

>*(***ANNA** *comes before the* **KING** *and curtseys. She wears a small bonnet.)*

KING. You are schoolteacher?

ANNA. Yes, Your Majesty. When may I start my work?

KING. I will tell you when I wish you to start.

ANNA. There is a matter we have to settle first, Your Majesty.

KING. *(Interrupting her.)* You are part of general plan I have for bringing to Siam what is good in Western culture. Already I have bring printing press here – for printing.

ANNA. Yes, I know, Your Majesty.

KING. How you know?

ANNA. Before I signed our agreement, I found out all I could about Your Majesty's ambitions for Siam.

KING. Ha! This is scientific.

(He squints at her thoughtfully.)

You are pleased with your apartments in Palace?

ANNA. They... are quite comfortable, Your Majesty.

(Exchanging a look with the **KRALAHOME.***)*

For the time being. But my young son and I have found it rather... confining... with Amazons guarding the doors and not permitting us to leave our quarters.

KING. Strangers cannot be allowed to roam around Palace before presentment to King. You could look out of windows.

ANNA. Yes, Your Majesty, we have done so. We have seen New Year celebrations, royal cremation ceremonies, etcetera, etcetera, etcetera.

KING. Etcetera! What is this "etcetera"?

ANNA. According to the dictionary, it means "and the rest" – all the things you have been doing while we have been waiting. The fireworks...

KING. Best fireworks I ever see at funeral. How you like my acrobats?

ANNA. Splendid, Your Majesty. Best acrobats I ever see at funeral.

KING. *(Pleased.)* Ha!

(To **KRALAHOME.***)*

Have children prepare for presentation to schoolteacher.

(The **KRALAHOME** *claps his hands and exits, followed by the two Amazons.)*

ANNA. How many children have you, Your Majesty?

KING. I have only sixty-seven altogether.

(A look of astonishment from **ANNA,** *The* **KING** *explains:)*

I begin very late. But you shall not teach all of them. You shall teach only children of mothers who are in favor with King...

*(***LADY THIANG*** enters.)*

Which at present are very few – very few indeed. Ah! Lady Thiang. Madame Leonowens. This is Lady Thiang, head wife.

*(***LADY THIANG*** starts to sing by rote.)*

MUSIC 7A: ["THERE IS A HAPPY LAND"]

LADY THIANG. *(Singing a cappella.)*
THERE IS A HAPPY LAND
FAR, FAR AWAY
WHERE SAINTS IN GLORY STAND
BRIGHT, BRIGHT AS DAY.

(Speaking.)

In the beginning God created the – heavens and the – earth.

*(***ANNA*** looks puzzled.)*

Mis-on-ary.

ANNA. A *missionary* taught you English!

LADY THIANG. Yes, sir. Mis-son-ary.

KING. Lady Thiang, you will help Madame Leonowens with her schoolteaching, and she in turn, will teach you the better English.

*(***LADY THIANG*** prostrates herself at the feet of the* **KING,** *to* **ANNA***'s surprise and horror. The* **KING** *explains:)*

She is grateful to me for my kindness.

ANNA. I see.

> (*Getting back to the issue she is anxious to settle.*)

Your Majesty, in our agreement, you...

KING. (*Talking across* ANNA.) You, Tuptim.

> (TUPTIM *rises.*)

You already speak well the English.

> (*The* KING *turns to* ANNA, *pointing to* TUPTIM.)

She arrived today. She is present to me from Burma prince.

ANNA. (*Shocked.*) *She* is a present?

TUPTIM. Madam, you have English books I can read?

ANNA. Of course I have.

TUPTIM. I wish most to read book called *The Small House of Uncle Thomas.* Is by American lady, Harriet Beecha Stowa.

KING. A woman has written a book?

ANNA. A very wonderful book, Your Majesty. An American book. All about slavery...

KING. Ha! President Lingkonk against slavery, no? Me, too. Slavery very bad thing.

> (ANNA *looks significantly at the prostrate figure of* LADY THIANG. *The* KING *snaps his fingers and* LADY THIANG *rises. The* KING *paces thoughtfully, speaking half to himself, half to* ANNA.)

I think you will teach my wives too – those wives who are in Royal favor.

(During the ensuing dialogue, small groups of the KING'S WIVES peek in through various entrances, curious, but afraid to be seen by the KING. When he turns in their direction they retreat and hide.)

ANNA. I shall be most happy to teach your wives, even though that was not part of our agreement... speaking of our agreement reminds me that there is one little matter, about my house...

(She takes the agreement letter from her handbag.)

KING. *(Crossing.)* Also, I will allow you to help me in my foreign correspondence.

ANNA. Yes, Your Majesty.

(Following him.)

I don't think you understand. Your Majesty, I don't think you understand about my house.

KING. *(Wheeling around suddenly.)* House? House? What is this about house.

ANNA. *(Startled, then recovering.)* I want my house.

(She indicates the agreement.)

The house you promised me, Your Majesty.

KING. *(Now he has been pushed to far.)* You shall live in Palace. You teach in Palace, you shall live in Palace. do not teach, and you go –

(He snatches the agreement letter from her outstretched hand.)

– wherever you please. I do not care.

(He turns and faces her.)

You understand this?

ANNA. Yes, Your Majesty. But if these are the only terms on which I am allowed to remain...

KING. Enough! I have no more time to talk. Talk to other women, my women – my wives.

> *(He snaps his fingers at* **TUPTIM**, *who follows him obediently as he exits. As soon as the* **KING** *has left, the* **WIVES** *rush on from all sides, chattering excitedly. They surround* **ANNA**, *taking her gloves and her reticule, fingering her clothes. Two on the floor try to lift up her skirt.)*

ANNA. For goodness sake! What is the matter? What are they trying to do to me?

LADY THIANG. They think you wear big skirt like that because you shaped like that.

ANNA. Well, look, I'm not!

> *(She lifts her hoop skirt, revealing pantalettes.)*

MUSIC 8: ["INCIDENTAL FOR DIALOGUE"]

> *(Two* **WIVES** *address* **LADY THIANG** *[measure 1], the orchestra once again playing sounds to indicate the Siamese language.)*

LADY THIANG. They wish to know, sir, if you have children?

ANNA. One little boy.

LADY THIANG. I have boy, too – Crown Prince Chaufa Chulalongkorn, heir to throne...

> *(An earnest pleading coming into her voice.)*

I would be happy if you would teach children.

ANNA. I would like to, very much. I came all the way here from Singapore to do so, but really... under these conditions...

LADY THIANG. You could be great help to all here, sir.

ANNA. Lady Thiang, why do you call me "sir"?

LADY THIANG. Because you scientific. Not lowly, like woman.

ANNA. Do you *all* think women are more lowly than men?

>   (**LADY THIANG** *translates this to the* **WIVES**
>   *[measure 2], all of whom smile broadly and
>   nod their heads happily [measure 6].* **ANNA***'s
>   voice is indignant.)*

Well, I don't.

LADY THIANG. Please sir, do not tell King. Make King very angry.

ANNA. King seems to be angry already.

>   *(Thoughtfully.)*

That lovely girl – He said she was a present...

LADY THIANG. From Prince of Burma. I think she love another man. If so, she will never see other man again.

ANNA. Poor child!

LADY THIANG. Oh no, sir. She is foolish child, to wish for another man when she has King.

ANNA. But you can't help wishing for a man, if he's the man you want.

LADY THIANG. It is strange for schoolteacher to talk so – romantic.

ANNA. Romantic! I suppose I am.

(She removes a locket from around her neck.)

I was very much in love with my late husband, Tom.

(She gives the locket to **LADY THIANG.***)*

LADY THIANG. Tom.

> *(Translating "Tom" to the wives [measure 8] she shows them the locket. They repeat after her, "Tom".)*

ANNA. Once a woman has loved like that, she understands all other women who are in love... and she's on their side too, even if she's... just a schoolteacher.

MUSIC 9: ["HELLO, YOUNG LOVERS"]

> *(On the downbeat of the music the wives again repeat "Tom" as if fascinated by the sound.)*

WIVES. Tom.

ANNA. Yes... Tom.

LADY THIANG. *(Looking at the picture and giving the locket back to* **ANNA.***)* He was pretty in face.

ANNA. *(Taking the locket.)* Oh dear, yes. He was very pretty in face.

> *(She sings, as one by one the* **WIVES** *slip slowly down to their knees and sit on their heels.)*

WHEN I THINK OF TOM
I THINK ABOUT A NIGHT
WHEN THE EARTH SMELLED OF SUMMER
AND THE SKY WAS STREAKED WITH WHITE
AND THE SOFT MIST OF ENGLAND
WAS SLEEPING ON A HILL,
I REMEMBER THIS
AND I ALWAYS WILL.

(LADY THIANG is the last to kneel.)

THERE ARE NEW LOVERS NOW ON THE SAME SILENT
   HILL,
LOOKING ON THE SAME BLUE SEA,
AND I KNOW TOM AND I ARE PART OF THEM ALL,
AND THEY'RE ALL A PART OF TOM AND ME.

*(She is far away from them now, in another
time, another place.)*

HELLO, YOUNG LOVERS,
WHOEVER YOU ARE,
I HOPE YOUR TROUBLES ARE FEW.
ALL MY GOOD WISHES GO WITH YOU TONIGHT,
I'VE BEEN IN LOVE LIKE YOU.

BE BRAVE, YOUNG LOVERS,
AND FOLLOW YOUR STAR,

**MUSIC 9A: ["HELLO, YOUNG LOVERS"] –
Encore**

BE BRAVE AND FAITHFUL AND TRUE.
CLING VERY CLOSE TO EACH OTHER TONIGHT,
I'VE BEEN IN LOVE LIKE YOU.

I KNOW HOW IT FEELS
TO HAVE WINGS ON YOUR HEELS
AND TO FLY DOWN A STREET IN A TRANCE.
YOU FLY DOWN A STREET
ON THE CHANCE THAT YOU'LL MEET,
AND YOU MEET NOT REALLY BY CHANCE.

DON'T CRY, YOUNG LOVERS,
WHATEVER YOU DO,
DON'T CRY BECAUSE I'M ALONE.
ALL OF MY MEMORIES
ARE HAPPY TONIGHT,
I'VE HAD A LOVE OF MY OWN.

I'VE HAD A LOVE OF MY OWN,
LIKE YOURS,
I'VE HAD A LOVE OF MY OWN.

> *(This encore should be included only when demanded by the audience.)*

MUSIC 10: ["GONG CUE"]

> *(The applause is broken by three loud gong crashes. The **KING** enters as the **WIVES** and **LADY THIANG** rise and take up kneeling positions in two lines, right.)*

KING. The children! The children! They come for presentment to schoolteacher.

> *(He mounts the dais.)*

ANNA. This is all very interesting, Your Majesty – but it has not solved my problem...

KING. Silence! You will stand here to meet Royal children.

> *(He indicates a place for her to stand, downstage left of the dais.)*

ANNA. *(Reluctantly accepting his order.)* Very well, Your Majesty.

KING. The Royal Princes and Princesses!

MUSIC 11: ["THE MARCH OF SIAMESE CHILDREN"]

> *(Now, to the strains of a patrol, the Royal Siamese **CHILDREN** enter, one by one, advancing first to the **KING** and prostrating themselves before him, then rising, moving over to **ANNA**, and greeting her in the traditional manner by taking her two hands and pressing them to their foreheads, after*

which they back away across the stage, and are placed by their respective mothers with the **CHILDREN** *who have previously entered. Each child enters at about the time that the preceeding child has greeted* **ANNA** *and is backing across the stage into position. The Twins enter together, and the* **KING** *holds up two fingers to* **ANNA**, *so that she is sure to observe that they are twins. There are other variations. One little girl goes straight to her father, her arms out-stretched, but he sternly points to the floor, She prostrates herself in the formal manner and, very much abashed, goes on to* **ANNA.** *Another little girl, who has been delegated to give* **ANNA** *a rose, forgets it the first time and has to run back to* **ANNA**, *disgraced by her absent-mindedness. The most impresssive moment is the entrance of the Crown Prince,* **CHULALONGKORN.** *The music [measure 53] becomes loud and brave at this point, and every move the Crown Prince makes is synchronized to it.* **CHULALONGKORN** *and the* **KING** *exchange ceremonious bows.* **CHULALONGKORN** *then moves to* **ANNA** *and waits for her reaction. Respectfully she acknowledges his rank with a full, formal curtsey.* **CHULALONGKORN** *in turn bows to her from the waist, fists on hips and feet apart, in the manner of his father.* **LADY THIANG** *shows her pride and indicates to* **ANNA** *that this is her son.* **CHULALONGKORN** *backs into position and kneels, a little in front of the others, downstage of* **LADY THIANG**, *who puts her arm around his shoulder. The patrol continues, diminishing in volume as the smallest child enters. On the last beat of the music the* **CHILDREN** *bow in unison. Throughout this procession,* **ANNA** *has obviously fallen more and more in love with them. She is deeply touched by their courtesy, their charm, their sweetness. After the applause, she slowly moves to the center of the room. She looks back at the* **KING,** *who nods understandingly, and then starts to untie the ribbons of her bonnet. She has decided to stay. As she takes out the pin and lifts the bonnet off her head the* **CHILDREN** *with one accord gasp an excited "Aah!" and rush up to her, surrounding her.)*

MUSIC 12: ["POSTLUDE TO THE MARCH OF SIAMESE CHILDREN"]

(She leans over and hugs all those she can reach. It is obvious that they are going to be fast friends as the music rises and the scene ends.)

Scene Four: The Palace Grounds

(A promenade (in one) among the buildings on the Palace Grounds, months later.)

(AT RISE: **PRIESTS** *enter, walking two by two and chanting in time to the music, their hands folded beneath their sleeves. They are followed by the* **CHILDREN,** *who enter walking normally and are singing. Behind them are* **CHULALONGKORN** *and* **PHRA ALACK,** *bringing up the rear.)*

MUSIC 13: ["SCENE BEFORE CURTAIN"]

PRIESTS. *(Chanting.)*
OH—
OH—
OH—

> *(They continue chanting as the* **CHILDREN** *sing.)*

CHILDREN. *(Singing.)*
BE IT EVER SO HUMBLE,
THERE'S NO PLACE LIKE HOME.
A CHARM FROM THE SKIES
SEEMS TO HALLOW US THERE,
WHICH, SEEN THROUGH THE WORLD,
IS NE'ER MET WITH ELSEWHERE.

> *(As they begin to exit, the* **KING** *enters.)*

KING. Chulalongkorn!

> *(The* **KING** *enters and gestures to* **CHULALONGKORN** *to step out of line. The* **PRINCE** *obeys. The* **PRIESTS** *and the other* **CHILDREN** *continue off-stage.)*

CHULALONGKORN. Father, I shall be late for school.

KING. *(Folding his arms.)* You wait!

> *(There is angry purpose in his voice and manner.)*

Please to recite proverb you have learned yesterday and writing down twelve times in your copybook.

CHULALONGKORN. *(Assuming the* **KING***'s stance.)* "A thought for the day: East or West, home is best."

KING. East, West, home best. Home! Means house. Every day for many, many months! Always something about a house! Are my children to be taught nothing more?

CHULALONGKORN. Yesterday we are taught that the world is a round ball which spins on a stick through the middle.

> *(He looks at the* **KING** *to see the effect of this outrageous statement.)*

Everyone knows that the world rides on the back of a great turtle, which keeps it from running into the stars.

KING. How *can* it be that everyone knows one thing, if many people believe another thing?

CHULALONGKORN. Then which is true?

> *(Pause.)*

KING. *(Decides hesitantly.)* The world is ball with stick through it... I believe.

CHULALONGKORN. You believe? Does that mean you do not *know*?

> *(His father does not answer.)*

But you must know, because you are King.

KING. Someday you too will be King and you too will know everything.

CHULALONGKORN. But how do I learn? And when do I know that I know everything?

KING. *(Not sure of himself.)* When – you – are – King. Now leave me.

> *(CHULALONGKORN goes out. The KING soliloquizes:)*

When you are King. But *I* do not know. I am not sure. I am not sure of anything.

MUSIC 14: ["A PUZZLEMENT"]

> *(He sings.)*

WHEN I WAS A BOY
WORLD WAS BETTER SPOT.
WHAT WAS SO WAS SO,
WHAT WAS NOT WAS NOT.

NOW I AM A MAN;
WORLD HAVE CHANGE A LOT.
SOME THINGS *NEARLY* SO,
OTHERS *NEARLY* NOT.

THERE ARE TIMES I ALMOST THINK
I AM NOT SURE OF WHAT I ABSOLUTELY KNOW.
VERY OFTEN FIND CONFUSION
IN CONCLUSION I CONCLUDED LONG AGO.
IN MY HEAD ARE MANY FACTS
THAT, AS A STUDENT, I HAVE STUDIED TO PROCURE.
IN MY HEAD ARE MANY FACTS
OF WHICH I WISH I WAS MORE CERTAIN I WAS SURE!

Is a puzzlement! What to tell a growing son?
WHAT, FOR INSTANCE, SHALL I SAY TO HIM OF WOMEN?
SHALL I EDUCATE HIM ON THE ANCIENT LINES?
SHALL I TELL THE BOY, AS FAR AS HE IS ABLE,

TO RESPECT HIS WIVES AND LOVE HIS CONCUBINES?
SHALL I TELL HIM EVERY ONE IS LIKE THE OTHER,
AND THE BETTER ONE OF TWO IS REALLY NEITHER?
IF I TELL HIM THIS I THINK HE WON'T BELIEVE IT,
AND I NEARLY THINK I DON'T BELIEVE IT EITHER!
WHEN MY FATHER WAS A KING
HE WAS A KING WHO KNEW EXACTLY WHAT HE KNEW,
AND HIS BRAIN WAS NOT A THING
FOREVER SWINGING TO AND FRO AND FRO AND TO.
SHALL I THEN BE LIKE MY FATHER
AND BE WILFULLY UNMOVABLE AND STRONG?
OR IS BETTER TO BE RIGHT?
OR AM I RIGHT WHEN I BELIEVE I MAY BE WRONG?
SHALL I JOIN WITH OTHER NATIONS IN ALLIANCE?
IF ALLIES ARE WEAK AM I NOT BEST ALONE?
IF ALLIES ARE STRONG WITH POWER TO PROTECT ME,
MIGHT THEY NOT PROTECT ME OUT OF ALL I OWN?
IS A DANGER TO BE TRUSTING ONE ANOTHER.
ONE WILL SELDOM WANT TO DO WHAT OTHER WISHES,
BUT UNLESS SOMEDAY SOMEBODY TRUST SOMEBODY
THERE'LL BE NOTHING LEFT ON EARTH EXCEPTING
     FISHES!
THERE ARE TIMES I ALMOST THINK
NOBODY SURE OF WHAT HE ABSOLUTELY KNOW.
EVERYBODY FIND CONFUSION
IN CONCLUSION HE CONCLUDED LONG AGO.
AND IT PUZZLE ME TO LEARN
THAT THO' A MAN MAY BE IN DOUBT OF WHAT HE KNOW,
VERY QUICKLY WILL HE FIGHT,
HE'LL FIGHT TO PROVE THAT WHAT HE DOES NOT KNOW
     IS SO!
OH-H-H-H-H-H!
SOMETIMES I THINK THAT PEOPLE GOING MAD!
AH-H-H-H-H-H!

SOMETIMES I THINK THAT PEOPLE NOT SO BAD.
BUT NO MATTER WHAT I THINK,
I MUST GO ON LIVING LIFE.
AS A LEADER OF MY KINGDOM I MUST GO FORTH;
BE FATHER TO MY CHILDREN,
AND HUSBAND TO EACH WIFE –
ETCETERA, ETCETERA, AND SO FORTH.

(His arms and eyes raised in prayer.)
IF MY LORD IN HEAVEN, BUDDHA, SHOW THE WAY,
EVERY DAY I TRY TO LIVE ANOTHER DAY.

(He drops forward onto his knees.)
IF MY LORD IN HEAVEN, BUDDHA, SHOW THE WAY,
EVERY DAY I DO MY BEST FOR ONE MORE DAY,

(His arms and shoulders droop. He sits back on his heels, speaking.)

BUT ...

(On the chord that follows he rises back up on his knees.)

IS A PUZZLEMENT!

(He opens his arms, clasps his hands back over his head and on the final glissando brings his head and hands to the floor. The lights go out. The voices of the CHILDREN are heard in the darkness, coming from the schoolroom.)

Scene Five: The Schoolroom

(The schoolroom, months later. Up center is a large stand with a map hanging from it. This is an ancient map, showing a very large Siam with a heroic figure of an armored king supreimposed. Adjoining is a much smaller Burma, with a pathetic naked figure representing the king of that country. There is a stool with a cushion on it to the left of the map.)

(AT RISE: The **CHILDREN** *are in diagonal lines up right of center, singing their school song. The* **WIVES** *are behind them.* **LADY THIANG** *and* **TUPTIM** *stand a little apart from the group, as does* **LOUIS**. **CHULALONGKORN** *is with the* **CHILDREN** *and* **WIVES**. *Amazons stand guard behind them.* **ANNA** *conducts them with a blackboard pointer. Soon after the curtain rises, she stops them in the middle of their song.)*

MUSIC 15: ["SCHOOLROOM SCENE"]

ALL.

WE WORK AND WORK
FROM WEEK TO WEEK
AT THE ROYAL BANGKOK ACADEMY,

AND ENGLISH WORDS
ARE ALL WE SPEAK
AT THE ROYAL BANGKOK ACADEMY ...

ANNA. *(Interupting them, the singing tails off, the music fades.)* Spread out, children.

(They obey, easing downstage.)

Now that last line was "English words are all we speak".
I didn't quite understand. I want to hear the beginnings
and ends of your words. Once again, now, and nice big
smiles, because we love our school. One, two, three.

ALL.
WE WORK AND WORK
FROM WEEK TO WEEK
AT THE ROYAL BANGKOK ACADEMY,

AND ENGLISH WORDS
ARE ALL WE SPEAK
AT THE ROYAL BANGKOK ACADEMY.

IF WE PAY ATTENTION TO OUR TEACHER
AND OBEY HER EVERY RULE,

WE'LL BE GRATEFUL FOR
THOSE GOLDEN YEARS
AT OUR DEAR OLD SCHOOL.

THE ROYAL BANGKOK ACADEMY,
OUR DEAR OLD SCHOOL.

ANNA. That's fine. Now, take you places for class. You all
know where you belong.

> *(The **CHILDREN** sit, the taller ones forming
> a diagonal on the right and the little ones
> forming a straight line down center, their
> backs to the audience and facing **ANNA**,
> who stands up center. The dancer who will
> perform the schoolroom dance with **ANNA**
> sits behind the **CHILDREN**. **TUPTIM** stands
> upstage of the dancer. **CHULALONGKORN**
> kneels upstage of **TUPTIM**. The Amazons move
> to each side of the map. The Amazon with
> the tray holding the finger cymbals **TUPTIM**
> will use later positions herself right of the
> map. **LOUIS** moves to up left of the map. The
> **WIVES** line up in two diagonal lines left, **LADY
> THIANG** to the left of the map.)*

Lady Thiang, will you start?

> (**ANNA** *hands the pointer to* **LADY THIANG** *and sits on the stool to the left of the map.*)

LADY THIANG. Blue is ocean. Red – Siam.

> (*Enthusiastic reaction from the* **CHILDREN** *at Siam's great size.*)

Here is King of Siam.

> (*Indicating armored figure.*)

In right hand is weapon – show how he destroy all who fight him.

> (*More approval.*)

Green – Burma.

> (**LADY THIANG** *looks disapprovingly at* **TUPTIM.**)

Here –

> (*Indicating naked figure.*)

is King of Burma. No clothes mean how poor is King of Burma.

> (**CHILDREN** *giggle.*)

ANNA. (*Taking the pointer from* **LADY THIANG.**) Thank you, Lady Thiang. Will you take my place?

> (**LADY THIANG** *sits.* **ANNA** *addresses the class:*)

The map you have been looking at is an old one. Today we have a surprise. Louis, –

> (**LOUIS** *rolls down an 1862 world map in Mercator projection. The* **CHILDREN** *gasp.*)

A new map – just arrived from England. It is a present to us from His Majesty, your King.

WIVES & CHILDREN. *(Dutifully.)* The Lord of light.

> *(They prostrate themselves.)*

ANNA. Er-yes – the Lord of light.

> *(They resume their positions as* **ANNA** *hands* **LOUIS** *the pointer.)*

LOUIS. *(With the pointer.)* The white is Siam.

> *(There is a groan of disbelief and disappointment from the* **CHILDREN** *and* **WIVES.***)*

CHULALONGKORN. *(Indignantly.)* Siam not so small!

ANNA. *(Aside to him.)* Hush, Your Highness!

LOUIS. Wait! Let me show you England.

> *(Points.)*

See! England is even smaller than Siam.

> *(The* **CHILDREN** *indicate their approval.* **LOUIS** *gives the pointer to* **LADY THIANG** *and places the stool center.* **LADY THIANG** *hangs the pointer on the back of the map stand.)*

ANNA. For many years, before I came here, Siam was to me just like that little white spot.

> *(She sits.)*

Now I have lived here for more than a year. I have met the people of Siam. I'm beginning to understand them.

A PRINCESS. You like us?

ANNA. I like you very much. Very much indeed.

MUSIC 16: ["GETTING TO KNOW YOU"]

CHILDREN. *(Expressing their delight.)* Ah!!!

ANNA. *(Speaking to the music.)*
IT'S A VERY ANCIENT SAYING,
BUT A TRUE AND HONEST THOUGHT,
THAT IF YOU BECOME A TEACHER
BY YOUR PUPILS YOU'LL BE TAUGHT.

> *(Singing.)*

AS A TEACHER I'VE BEEN LEARNING,
(YOU'LL FORGIVE ME IF I BOAST)
AND I'VE NOW BECOME AN EXPERT
ON THE SUBJECT I LIKE MOST:

> *(She speaks.)*

Getting to know you.

> *(The **CHILDREN** giggle. She sings.)*

GETTING TO KNOW YOU,
GETTING TO KNOW ALL ABOUT YOU.
GETTING TO LIKE YOU,
GETTING TO HOPE YOU LIKE ME.

GETTING TO KNOW YOU,
PUTTING IT MY WAY,
BUT NICELY,
YOU ARE PRECISELY

> *(She holds her arm up, gesturing as if she were holding a teacup.)*

MY CUP OF TEA!

GETTING TO KNOW YOU,
GETTING TO FEEL FREE AND EASY.
WHEN I AM WITH YOU,
GETTING TO KNOW WHAT TO SAY.
HAVEN'T YOU NOTICED?

SUDDENLY I'M BRIGHT AND BREEZY
BECAUSE OF
ALL THE BEAUTIFUL AND NEW
THINGS I'M LEARNING ABOUT YOU
DAY
BY
DAY.

(The refrain is taken up by the **WIVES** *and Amazons.* **ANNA** *crosses down to the front line of smaller* **CHILDREN** *right and begins teaching them how to shake hands.* **LOUIS** *replaces stool up left of the map. Then he crosses to the diagonal of taller* **CHILDREN** *right and teaches them handshaking.)*

ALL (EXCEPT CHILDREN).
GETTING TO KNOW YOU,
GETTING TO KNOW ALL ABOUT YOU.
GETTING TO LIKE YOU,
GETTING TO HOPE YOU LIKE ME.

(As **ANNA** *reaches the twins she is a little perplexed by the fact that they are, as always, holding hands. She solves this problem of their handshake by crossing her own hands. She then encourages the* **WIVES** *to join in shaking hands. They do.)*

GETTING TO KNOW YOU,
PUTTING IT MY WAY,
BUT NICELY,
YOU ARE PRECISELY

(The **CHILDREN** *reach towards her with both arms.)*

ANNA. MY CUP OF TEA!

(On the word "tea" all **CHILDREN** *respond with a salaam.)*

ALL.

GETTING TO KNOW YOU,
GETTING TO FEEL FREE AND EASY.

*(***ANNA*** *curtsies to* **LADY THIANG. LADY THIANG** *imitates her.* **LOUIS** *bows to* **CHULALONGKORN. CHULALONGKORN** *imitates him.)*

WHEN I AM WITH YOU,
GETTING TO KNOW WHAT TO SAY.

*(***ANNA, LOUIS, LADY THIANG*** *and* **CHULALONGKORN** *form a "wheel" and do a short minuet turn.)*

HAVEN'T YOU NOTICED?
SUDDENLY I'M BRIGHT AND BREEZY
BECAUSE OF
ALL THE BEAUTIFUL AND NEW
THINGS I'M LEARNING ABOUT YOU

*(***ANNA*** *turns to shake the hand of a small boy who has been tugging on her skirt. He then gives her his hat.)*

DAY
BY
DAY.

(Schoolroom dance – the twins run up to get the dancer and bring her forward [measure 88]. The **CHILDREN** *clear left and right.* **TUPTIM** *takes up position with finger cymbals to the right of the map. The dancer dances with her fan [measure 90] as* **ANNA** *and the others watch. At [measure 106] the* **CHILDREN** *push* **ANNA** *forward to join the dancer. As she does so the dancer tosses her fan to* **ANNA** *and*

takes a second fan from her belt. **ANNA** *and the dancer dance with their fans as the* **WIVES** *and* **CHILDREN** *sing [measure 107].)*

WIVES & CHILDREN. *(As they sing* **ANNA** *sways her skirt. The dancer, realizing she doesn't have a skirt, calls four* **CHILDREN** *around her to be her "skirt".)*
GETTING TO KNOW YOU,
GETTING TO FEEL FREE AND EASY.
WHEN I AM WITH YOU,
GETTING TO KNOW WHAT TO SAY.

> *(***ANNA*** and the dancer step left. The dancer's "skirt" "forgets" to move with her and has to scurry to catch up with her.)*

HAVEN'T YOU NOTICED?
SUDDENLY I'M BRIGHT AND BREEZY
BECAUSE OF
ALL THE BEAUTIFUL AND NEW
THINGS I'M LEARNING ABOUT YOU
DAY
BY
DAY.

ANNA. *(Sitting down center and tapping her fan left and right, she summons the* **CHILDREN** *to her side. One by one they join her, facing front.)*

> *(After applause.)*

MUSIC 17: ["GETTING TO KNOW YOU"] – Encore

> *(This encore should be included only when demanded by the audience.)*

GETTING TO KNOW YOU,
GETTING TO FEEL FREE AND EASY.
WHEN I AM WITH YOU,
GETTING TO KNOW WHAT TO SAY.

HAVEN'T YOU NOTICED?
SUDDENLY I'M BRIGHT AND BREEZY

ALL.
BECAUSE OF
ALL THE BEAUTIFUL AND NEW
THINGS I'M LEARNING ABOUT YOU
DAY
BY
DAY.

ANNA. My goodness! This started out to be a lesson! Now let's get back to work. Now, are there any questions?

> *(They scurry back to their places.)*

CHULALONGKORN. *(Pointing to the map.)* What is that green up there?

ANNA. That is Norway.

> *(Repeating precisely for the benefit of her students.)*

Nor-way.

WIVES & CHILDREN. *(Imitating the sound.)* Norway.

ANNA. Norway is a very cold place. It is sometimes so cold that the lakes and rivers freeze, and the water becomes so hard you can walk on it.

A SMALL PRINCE. Walk on water?

ANNA. Yes, walk on water.

CHULALONGKORN. *(Incredulous.)* How is possible? Hard water!

ANNA. It is not only hard, but very slippery too. When people walk on it, they fall down, and slide...

> *(General reaction of skepticism.)*

Not only do the lakes and rivers freeze, but the raindrops, as they fall, are changed into small white spots that look like lace! This is called snow!

TUPTIM. *(Fascinated.)* Snow?

CHULALONGKORN. *(All but sneering.)* Spots of lace!

> *(The CHILDREN giggle, their credulity strained. The class decorum begins to unravel.)*

ANNA. Yes, Your Highness! The water freezes – on the way down from the sky.

CHULALONGKORN. And the raindrops turn into little stars!

ANNA. Yes, Your Highness. Some *are* shaped like stars – small, white –

> *(Bedlam is threatening.)*

FIRST PRINCESS. There's not a word of truth in it.

PRINCESS YING YAOWLAK. I do not believe such thing as snow!

> *(Cries of assent.)*

FIRST PRINCESS. And I do not believe Siam is so big –

> *(Indicating size with her hands.)*

SECOND PRINCESS. And other countries *so* big.

> *(Making an even wider gesture.)*

CHULALONGKORN. Siam biggest country in the world!

> *(Pandemonium breaks loose – Shouts and cartwheels greet this popular pronouncement.)*

KING. *(Entering suddenly.)* What? What? What?

(All but **ANNA** *and* **LOUIS** *instantly prostrate themselves. The* **KING** *stands for a moment in outraged silence.)*

How can schoolroom be so... unscientific?

ANNA. Your Majesty, we have had a little misunderstanding. I was describing snow to them and they refused to believe that there was such a thing.

KING. Snow?

ANNA. *(Gesturing snow falling.)* Snow.

> *(***CHULALONGKORN*** *has raised his head and noted her gesture.)*

KING. *(Feeling his way.)* Ah, yes, from mountain top.

ANNA. From the sky.

KING. From sky *to* mountain top.

CHULALONGKORN. *(Kneels up.)* Sire... please... How does it come down from the sky?

KING. *(He looks at* **ANNA** *for guidance. Surreptitiously she raises her right hand, then lowers it as she wriggles her fingers, making a falling leaf gesture. The* **KING** *looks at* **CHULALONGKORN** *and makes exactly the same gesture.)* Like this.

CHULALONGKORN. *(Gravely.)* Thank you, sire.

> *(He resumes his head down position.)*

KING. *(He snaps his fingers as if bringing the picture back to his mind.)* I have seen pictures – Switzerland! Land all white – with snow.

ANNA. That's right, Your Majesty.

> *(All heads slowly start to rise.)*

KING. *(Turning to the class, with an angry challenge.)* Who does not believe this?

(All heads duck quickly. There is complete silence.)

ANNA. Well, after all, they have never *seen* it.

KING. Never see? If they will know only what they see, why do we have schoolroom?

> *(He turns to the class and crackles out a sudden command.)*

Rise!

> *(They all come to their feet.)*

Do not ever let me hear of not believing schoolteacher whom I have bring here at great expense – twenty pounds –

> *(They all gasp as if she were robbing the* KING.*)*

Each month!

> *(Another gasp. All eyes turn toward* ANNA *with a strange accusing look.)*

Twenty English pounds!

> *(He stamps his foot.)*

Sterling!

> *(Not knowing what "sterling" means, but impressed by the sound as the* KING *shouts it, they all fall to the floor again.)*

Children must learn.

> *(He turns to* ANNA.*)*

Teacher must teach! Not waste time instructing children in silly English song "Home, Sweet House" – to remind me of breaking promises I never made, etcetera, etcetera, etcetera –

ANNA. *(Summoning all her courage.)* Your Majesty... you *did* promise me a house.

> *(He glares at her, but she does not flinch.)*

"A brick residence adjoining the Royal Palace." Those were your words in your letter.

KING. I do not remember such words.

ANNA. I remember them.

KING. *I* will do remembering. Who is King here. I remind you – so you remember *that*!

> *(Almost shouting.)*

I do not know of any promises. I do not know anything except that you are my servant.

ANNA. *(Automatically resenting the word.)* Oh, no, Your Majesty!

> *(There is a gasp of astonishment from those in the schoolroom. Heads rise.)*

KING. What? What? What? I say you are my servant!

> (CHULALONGKORN *moves to his father's side.)*

ANNA. No, Your Majesty, indeed – I am *not* your servant.

> (LOUIS *moves to his mother's side.)*

CHULALONGKORN. *(To* LOUIS.*)* I would say your mother has bad manners.

LOUIS. *(Hotly.)* Oh, you would, would you? Well, I'd say your father has no manners at all!

(Both boys move towards each other to fight. Both are restrained by their respective parents. Abashedly, CHULALONGKORN resumes a kneeling position.)

ANNA. Louis!

(She takes his hand and turns to face the KING.)

If you do not give me the house you promised me, I shall return to England.

(There is a frightened murmur from the CHILDREN. ANNA, herself, looks surprised at her own temerity.)

CHILDREN. *(Overlapping.)* No! No! No! Do not go to England.

A PRINCESS. We learn. We believe schoolteacher.

PRINCESS YING YAOWLAK. *(Crawling on her knees to the KING.)* I believe in snow!

LADY THIANG. *(To the KING.)* Do not let her go away.

KING. *(Firmly, confidently.)* I let her do nothing that is not my pleasure.

(To ANNA.)

It is my pleasure you stay here. You stay here in Palace.

(Facing front, arms folded.)

In Palace!

ANNA. No, Your Majesty!

KING. *(Weakening a little, he cajoles her.)* I give you servants. I give you bigger room.

(He eases himself between two of the CHILDREN.)

ANNA. *(Not weakening.)* That is not the point, Your Majesty.

KING. *(Placing his hands on the heads of the two* CHILDREN *he is now standing between.)* Why wish you to leave these children, all whom loving you so extraordinarily?

ANNA. *(Looking at the twins and then at* CHULALONGKORN.*)* I do not wish to leave them. I love them too... quite extraordinarily. But I cannot stay in a country where a promise has no meaning.

KING. *(Angrily.)* I will hear no more about this promise...

ANNA. A land where there is talk of honor, and a wish for Siam to take her place among the modern nations of the world! Where there is talk of great changes, but where everything still remains according to the wishes of the King!

KING. *(Threateningly.)* You will say *no more!*

ANNA. *(On the edge of tears.)* I will say no more, because – I have no more to say.

    (She starts off.)

Come, Louis.

    (He follows her out.)

WIVES AND CHILDREN. *(They call after her, their pleas overlapping, but she goes. .)* Please don't go, Mrs. Anna! Please, Mrs. Anna.

    (The KING *stamps his foot angrily to silence them all.)*

KING. Out! Out! Out!

    (They scurry out, left and right. The KING *crosses down right center and faces upstage.* CHULALONGKORN *and* LADY THIANG *have remained kneeling left and right of the* KING.

LADY THIANG *kneels up and makes a gesture of appeal to him. The* KING *dismisses her with a curt movement of his head. She backs off left and exits as* CHULALONGKORN *backs off and exits right. The* KING *is alone. His thoughts are confused. He paces up and down, then crosses up to right of map and looks at it.)*

MUSIC 18: ["INCIDENTAL"]

(His voice is low and thoughtful [measure 2].) So Big a World! Siam very small... England very small... All people very small. No man big enough for to be alone. No man big enough!

[Music measure 6.]

King different! King need no one... nobody at all!

[Music measure 8.]

I think!

[Music measure 100.]

(He leaves the room.)

(In a moment TUPTIM *comes in [measure 12]. She looks around cautiously, then assumes a kneeling position, sitting on her knees, left of center. She opens a book, pretending to read.* LUN THA *enters, [measure 14] then stops quickly, surprised to find* TUPTIM *alone.)*

LUN THA. Where is Mrs. Anna?

TUPTIM. She will not be with us ever again. She has quarreled with the King.

LUN THA. How can we meet, if she is not with us? Mrs. Anna was our only friend...

(He moves towards her.)

TUPTIM. We cannot be seen talking like this. Anyone can come in. Pretend you wait for her.

> *(He assumes a kneeling position right of center. Knowing they can not be seen together there is a palpable distance between them.)*

MUSIC 19: ["WE KISS IN A SHADOW"]

LUN THA. *(Bitterly.)* If only we could stop pretending.

> *(He sings.)*

WE KISS IN A SHADOW,
WE HIDE FROM THE MOON.
OUR MEETINGS ARE FEW
AND OVER TOO SOON.

WE SPEAK IN A WHISPER,
AFRAID TO BE HEARD.
WHEN PEOPLE ARE NEAR
WE SPEAK NOT A WORD.

ALONE IN OUR SECRET,
TOGETHER WE SIGH
FOR ONE SMILING DAY
TO BE FREE,

TO KISS IN THE SUNLIGHT
AND SAY TO THE SKY:
BEHOLD AND BELIEVE WHAT YOU SEE!
BEHOLD HOW MY LOVER LOVES ME!

> *(**LUN THA**, cautious and tense, backs upstage, looks first right and then left and then comes down slowly to **TUPTIM** from behind. He stops short of embracing her, knowing he can not. Their faces register their longing.)*

Tuptim, when can we meet? When?

TUPTIM. It is not possible. We cannot meet alone – not ever.

> *(Although they long to touch, they do not, knowing what the consequences would be. She sings.)*

WE SPEAK IN A WHISPER,
AFRAID TO BE HEARD,
WHEN PEOPLE ARE NEAR
WE SPEAK NOT A WORD.

LUN THA.

ALONE IN OUR SECRET,
TOGETHER WE SIGH
FOR ONE SMILING DAY
TO BE FREE,

BOTH.

TO KISS IN THE SUNLIGHT
AND SAY TO THE SKY:
BEHOLD AND BELIEVE WHAT YOU SEE!
BEHOLD HOW MY LOVER LOVES ME!

> *(During the applause the music resumes again [pick up to measure 77]. LUN THA and TUPTIM hold their positions, their faces and bodies betraying their intense feelings as they draw closer to each other. LADY THIANG enters from up left, sees them, backs off, comes back onstage to be sure, and backs offstage again, unseen by the two lovers. LUN THA is about to kiss TUPTIM. Suddenly she breaks away.)*

LUN THA. What is it?

TUPTIM. Someone was here!

> *(She looks around fearfully.)*

I had a feeling someone was watching us... Please go!
Please!

    *(***LUN THA** *leaves.* **TUPTIM** *sings sadly.)*

TO KISS IN THE SUNLIGHT
AND SAY TO THE SKY:
BEHOLD AND BELIEVE WHAT YOU SEE!
BEHOLD HOW MY LOVER LOVES ME!

Scene Six: A Palace Corridor

(The Palace corridor (in one), immediately following.)

MUSIC 20: ["A PUZZLEMENT"] – Reprise

(AT RISE: **LOUIS** *and* **CHULALONGKORN** *enter from opposite sides, in time to the music. They see each other, fold their arms and cross to opposite sides of the stage, snubbing each other. Then, with a common impulse, each repents and turns, running and meeting center stage and shaking hands [measure 17]. The music fades as they speak.)*

CHULALONGKORN. I am sorry we nearly fought just now.

LOUIS. I am too.

CHULALONGKORN. Are you really going away?

LOUIS. Mother plans to leave on the next sailing.

CHULALONGKORN. I am not sure my father will *allow* your mother to go.

LOUIS. I am not sure whether my mother will allow your father *not* to allow her to go.

CHULALONGKORN. Why does not your mother admit that she was *wrong*?

LOUIS. I don't believe that mother thinks she *was* wrong.

*(**LOUIS** faces **CHULALONGKORN** agressively. Almost nose to nose they raise their fists, but think the better of it and relax.)*

CHULALONGKORN. *(Thoughtfully.)* It begins to look as if people do not know when they are right or wrong – even after they have grown up.

LOUIS. I have noticed that too.

> *(Music begins again [pick-up to measure 37].)*

CHULALONGKORN. A puzzlement! ...When I left my father a little while ago, I heard him talking to himself. He seemed uncertain about many things.

LOUIS. I don't believe grown-ups are very certain – they only talk as if they are certain.

CHULALONGKORN. *(Singing:)*
THERE ARE TIMES I ALMOST THINK
THEY ARE NOT SURE OF WHAT THEY ABSOLUTELY KNOW.

LOUIS.
I BELIEVE THEY ARE CONFUSED
ABOUT CONCLUSIONS THEY CONCLUDED LONG AGO.

CHULALONGKORN.
IF MY FATHER AND YOUR MOTHER ARE NOT SURE
OF WHAT THEY ABSOLUTELY KNOW,
CAN YOU TELL ME WHY THEY FIGHT?

LOUIS.
THEY FIGHT TO PROVE THAT WHAT THEY
DO NOT KNOW IS SO!

CHULALONGKORN. *(With the gestures of his father.)*
OH-H-H-H-H-H!
SOMETIMES I THINK THAT PEOPLE GOING MAD!

LOUIS.
AH-H-H-H-H-H!
SOMETIMES I THINK THAT PEOPLE NOT SO BAD.

CHULALONGKORN.
BUT NO MATTER WHAT I THINK
I MUST GO ON LIVING LIFE,
AND SOME DAY AS A LEADER I MUST GO FORTH;

BE FATHER TO MY CHILDREN.
AND HUSBAND TO EACH WIFE.
ETCETERA, ETCETERA,
AND SO FORTH.

(His eyes and arms uplifted.)

IF MY LORD IN HEAVEN, BUDDHA, SHOW THE WAY,
EVERY DAY I TRY TO LIVE ANOTHER DAY.

(He drops to his knees.)

IF MY LORD IN HEAVEN, BUDDHA, SHOW THE WAY,
EVERY DAY I DO MY BEST FOR ONE MORE DAY!
BUT...

*(**LOUIS** crosses to stand behind* **CHULALONGKORN.***)*

LOUIS. *(With his hands on his hips.)*
IS A PUZZLEMENT!

(The two boys walk off together, arms around each other's shoulders.)

Scene Seven: Anna's Bedroom

(**ANNA**'s bedroom, that evening. There is a
single size Victorian spool bed center, covered
by a patchwork quilt and a plain bolster. An
old fashioned man's watch and chain are
hanging from the downstage left bedpost. To
the right of the bed is a small teak table on
which stands a lighted bed lamp. Left of the
bed is a four-fold Chinese laquered screen, on
which is hanging **ANNA**'s woollen shawl. At
the doorway right hangs a string of bells.)

**MUSIC 21: ["SHALL I TELL YOU WHAT I
THINK OF YOU?"]**

(AT RISE: **ANNA** is lying on the bed. She
has started to undress, but, engrossed in her
thoughts, has apparently stopped. Suddenly
[measure 10] she sits up. She glares scornfully
at an imaginary adversary downstage right.
Then, fuming, she lets him have it:)

ANNA. (Parlando [spoken to music].)
YOUR SERVANT! YOUR SERVANT!
INDEED I'M NOT YOUR SERVANT
(ALTHOUGH YOU GIVE ME LESS THAN SERVANT'S PAY)
I'M A FREE AND INDEPENDENT EMPLOYÉ –

(Correcting herself.)
EMPLOYEE.

(She paces the floor indignantly, then turns
back to "him".)
BECAUSE I'M A WOMAN
YOU THINK, LIKE EV'RY WOMAN,
I HAVE TO BE A SLAVE OR CONCUBINE –
YOU CONCEITED, SELF-INDULGENT LIBERTINE –

(She pronounces it with a long "I", correcting her pronunciation to a short "I".)

LIBERTINE.

(Narrowing her eyes vindictively, she sings.)

HOW I WISH I'D CALLED HIM THAT,
RIGHT TO HIS FACE!

(Parlando.)

LIBERTINE!

(Turning and addressing "him" again, singing.)

AND WHILE WE'RE ON THE SUBJECT, SIRE,
THERE ARE CERTAIN GOINGS ON
AROUND THIS PLACE
THAT I WISH
TO TELL YOU I DO NOT ADMIRE:
I DO NOT LIKE POLYGAMY
OR EVEN MODERATE BIGAMY.
(I REALIZE
THAT IN YOUR EYES
THAT CLEARLY MAKES A PRIG O' ME)
BUT I AM FROM A CIVILIZED LAND CALLED WALES,

(Giving a British salute, parlando.)

WHERE MEN LIKE YOU ARE KEPT IN COUNTY JAILS!

(Singing.)

IN YOUR PURSUIT OF PLEASURE, YOU
HAVE MISTRESSES WHO TREASURE YOU.
(THEY HAVE NO KEN
OF OTHER MEN
BESIDE WHOM THEY CAN MEASURE YOU)
A FLOCK OF SHEEP, AND YOU ARE THE ONLY RAM –

(Parlando.)

NO WONDER YOU'RE THE WONDER OF SIAM!

(At first elated by this sally a frightened, embarrassed look comes into her eyes. She speaks.)

I'm rather glad I *didn't* say that... Not with the women right there... and the children.

(She sings wistfully.)

THE CHILDREN, THE CHILDREN,
I'LL NOT FORGET THE CHILDREN.
NO MATTER WHERE I GO I'LL ALWAYS SEE
THOSE LITTLE FACES LOOKING UP AT ME ...

(She sits.)

AT FIRST, WHEN I STARTED TO TEACH,
THEY WERE SHY AND REMAINED OUT OF REACH,
BUT LATELY I'VE THOUGHT
ONE OR TWO HAVE BEEN CAUGHT
BY A WORD I HAVE SAID
OR A SENTENCE I'VE READ,
AND I'VE HEARD AN OCCASIONAL QUESTION
THAT IMPLIED, AT THE LEAST, A SUGGESTION
THAT THE WORK I WAS TRYING TO DO
WAS BEGINNING TO SHOW WITH A FEW!
THAT PRINCE CHULALONGKORN
IS VERY LIKE HIS FATHER.
HE'S STUBBORN – BUT INQUISITIVE AND SMART...

(Suddenly emotional.)

I MUST LEAVE THIS PLACE BEFORE THEY BREAK MY
      HEART,

(Rising.)

I MUST LEAVE THIS PLACE BEFORE THEY BREAK MY
      HEART!

(She stops, bites her lip and looks at the watch that is hanging on her bedpost.)

Goodness! I had no idea it was so late!

(She is about to resume undressing, but instead hitches her corset as if she were girding her loins and is back at the "KING" again.)

(Beginning a slow boil, parlando.)
SHALL I TELL YOU WHAT I THINK OF YOU?
YOU'RE SPOILED!
YOU'RE A CONSCIENTIOUS WORKER,
BUT YOU'RE SPOILED.

(Singing.)
GIVING CREDIT WHERE IT'S DUE
THERE IS MUCH I LIKE IN YOU,
BUT IT'S ALSO VERY TRUE

(Spoken.)

THAT YOU'RE SPOILED!

(She struts up and down, imitating him, parlando.)
EVERYBODY'S ALWAYS BOWING

(As if she were toasting him.)
TO THE KING!
EVERYBODY HAD TO GROVEL

(Another toast.)
TO THE KING!

(Singing.)
BY YOUR BUDDHA YOU ARE BLESSED,
BY YOUR LADIES YOU'RE CARESSED,

BUT THE ONE WHO LOVES YOU BEST
(IS THE KING!)

> *(She pantomimes the last three words by poking a mocking finger at the imaginary "KING" on these three beats.)*

> *(Parlando.)*

ALL THAT BOWING AND KOW-TOWING
TO REMIND YOU OF YOUR ROYALTY,
I FIND A MOST DISGUSTING EXHIBITION.

> *(On the music cue [measure 189] she falls on her face in a mock salaam gesture, then sits up, continuing.)*

I WOULDN'T ASK A SIAMESE CAT
TO DEMONSTRATE HIS LOYALTY
BY TAKING THIS RIDICULOUS POSITION.

> *(She falls forward on her hands and knees, [measure 193] looking up front.)*

HOW WOULD YOU LIKE IT IF YOU WERE A MAN
PLAYING THE PART OF A TOAD?

> *(To illustrate the point she crawls around until she is again facing front on her elbows and knees.)*

CRAWLING AROUND ON YOUR ELBOWS AND KNEES,
EATING THE DUST IN THE ROAD!

> *(She sits up.)*

TOADS! TOADS!

> *(To the "KING".)*

ALL OF YOUR PEOPLE ARE TOADS!
YES, YOUR MAJESTY! NO, YOUR MAJESTY!
TELL US HOW LOW TO GO, YOUR MAJESTY!
MAKE SOME MORE DECREES, YOUR MAJESTY!

DON'T LET US UP OFF OUR KNEES, YOUR MAJESTY!
GIVE US A KICK, IF IT PLEASE, YOUR MAJESTY!
GIVE US A KICK, IF YOU *WOULD*, YOUR MAJESTY!

> *(She reacts to "taking" an imaginary kick from the "KING".)*

Oh, that was *good*, <u>Your Majesty</u>!

> *(She pounds the floor in her temper, then lies prone, exhausted, as the music ends. As the applause subsides* **LADY THIANG** *rings the doorbell timidly.* **ANNA**, *only half believing that she has heard the bell, lifts her head and listens.* **LADY THIANG** *rings again.)*

ANNA. *(Startled.)* Who is it?

LADY THIANG. Mrs. Anna, it is I, Lady Thiang.

ANNA. At this hour of the night! One moment, Lady Thiang.

> *(***ANNA** *rises, and gets her shawl from the screen. She opens the door, putting the shawl around her shoulders as she does so.* **LADY THIANG** *enters.)*

LADY THIANG. Mrs. Anna, will you go to King?

ANNA. Now? Has he sent for me?

LADY THIANG. *(A pause, then:)* No. But he would be glad to see you.

> *(***ANNA**, *scornful, moves away from her.)*

He is deeply wounded man. No one has ever spoken to him as you did today in schoolroom.

ANNA. Lady Thiang, no one has ever behaved to *me* as His Majesty did today in the schoolroom!

LADY THIANG. And there is more distressing thing. Our agents in Singapore have found letters to British Government from certain people whose greedy eyes are on Siam. They describe King as barbarian, and suggest making Siam protectorate.

ANNA. That is outrageous! He is many things I do not like, but he is not a barbarian.

LADY THIANG. Then you will help him?

ANNA. You mean – advise him?

LADY THIANG. *(Tactful.)* It must not sound like advice. King cannot take advice. And if you go to him, he will not bring up subject. You must bring it up.

ANNA. I cannot go to him. It's against all my principles. Certainly not without him having *asked* for me.

LADY THIANG. He wish to be new-blood King with Western ideas. But it is hard for him, Mrs. Anna. And there is something else – Princess Tuptim. I do not tell King this for his sake. This I will deal with in my own way. But for these other things, he need help, Mrs. Anna.

ANNA. He has *you*.

LADY THIANG. I am not equal to his special needs. He could be great man. But he need special help. He need *you*.

(She crosses to **ANNA** *and touches her hands.)*

ANNA. *(Drawing back.)* Lady Thiang, please don't think I'm just being stubborn. But I cannot go to him. I *will* not.

MUSIC 22: ["SOMETHING WONDERFUL"]

LADY THIANG. *(Frustrated.)* What more can I say to you?

(She sings.)

THIS IS A MAN WHO THINKS WITH HIS HEART,

HIS HEART IS NOT ALWAYS WISE.
THIS IS A MAN WHO STUMBLES AND FALLS,
BUT THIS IS A MAN WHO TRIES.
THIS IS A MAN YOU'LL FORGIVE AND FORGIVE,
AND HELP AND PROTECT, AS LONG AS YOU LIVE ...

HE WILL NOT ALWAYS SAY
WHAT YOU WOULD HAVE HIM SAY,
BUT NOW AND THEN HE'LL SAY
SOMETHING WONDERFUL.

THE THOUGHTLESS THINGS HE'LL DO
WILL HURT AND WORRY YOU,
THEN ALL AT ONCE HE'LL DO
SOMETHING WONDERFUL.

HE HAS A THOUSAND DREAMS
THAT WON'T COME TRUE.
YOU KNOW THAT HE BELIEVES IN THEM,
AND THAT'S ENOUGH FOR YOU.

YOU'LL ALWAYS GO ALONG,
DEFEND HIM WHEN HE'S WRONG,
AND TELL HIM, WHEN HE'S STRONG,
HE IS WONDERFUL.

(She looks directly at **ANNA**.*)*

HE'LL ALWAYS NEED YOUR LOVE,
AND SO HE'LL GET YOUR LOVE –
A MAN WHO NEEDS YOUR LOVE
CAN BE WONDERFUL.

(As she finishes she kneels and looks up at **ANNA** *suppliantly.)*

MUSIC 23: ["CHANGE OF SCENE (PANTOMIME)"]

*(***ANNA** *looks down at her and nods understandingly, "Yes, she will go."* **LADY THIANG** *smiles.* **ANNA** *takes her hand and*

helps her rise. Then she crosses to the bed, picks up her jacket and starts to put it on. **LADY THIANG,** *taking this as a sign that her mission is successful, smiles gratefully and leaves* **ANNA** *to finish dressing.)*

Scene Eight: A Palace Corridor

(The Palace corridor (in one), immediately following.)

MUSIC 24: ["SOMETHING WONDERFUL"] – Reprise

(LADY THIANG, exiting ANNA's bedroom, comes down into one in front of the corridor drop. She crosses to meet the KRALAHOME, who has been pacing up and down the corridor, worried.)

KRALAHOME. Did you succeed? Will she go to him?

LADY THIANG. She will go. She knows he needs her. Tell him.

KRALAHOME. I will tell him she is anxious to come. I will tell him it is *she* who needs *him.*

LADY THIANG. That also will be true.

(The KRALAHOME leaves her. LADY THIANG soliloquizes:)

This woman knows many things, but this I think she does not know...

(She sings.)

SHE'LL ALWAYS GO ALONG,
DEFEND HIM WHEN HE'S WRONG,
AND TELL HIM WHEN HE'S STRONG,
HE IS WONDERFUL.

HE'LL ALWAYS NEED HER LOVE,
AND SO HE'LL GET HER LOVE –
A MAN WHO NEEDS YOUR LOVE
CAN BE WONDERFUL.

(She exits right on applause.)

MUSIC 25: ["CHANGE OF SCENE (POSTLUDE TO "SOMETHING WONDERFUL")"]

Scene Nine: The King's Library

*(The **KING**'s library, immediately following. Next to the dais is a gong hung in a frame with a soft stick. There is a throw rug and an arm-rest pillow on the floor, a large English Bible with a pair of spectacles set between its open pages on the rug. A notebook with a pencil on a chain has been set on the dais. There are English newspapers strewn about.)*

*(AT RISE: The **KING** is walking up and down impatiently. He goes up and out to the terrace, looks off left, sees **ANNA** approaching, hurries down to the arm pillow, puts on his spectacles and resumes reading the Bible. In a moment, **ANNA** enters, stands at the top of the terrace stairs, takes in the scene and curtseys.)*

ANNA. Your Majesty.

(She comes into the room and curtseys again.)

Your Majesty.

*(He pretends not to hear her. He leans closer to his book. The music fades. **ANNA** comes downstage, level with him, and peers over his shoulder at the book.)*

Your Majesty is reading the Bible!

KING. *(Remaining on the floor, pretending great surprise.)* Ah! Mrs. Anna. I think your Moses shall have been a fool.

ANNA. Moses?

KING. *(Impatiently, as he sits up.)* Moses! Moses! Moses!

(Tapping the Bible.)

Here it stands written by him that the world was created in six days! You know and I know it took many ages to create world. I think he shall have been a fool to have written so. What is your opinion?

ANNA. Your Majesty, the Bible was not written by men of science, but by men of faith.

> (*The* KING *considers this. Removing his glasses, he places them on the Bible.*)

It was their explanation of the miracle of creation, which is the same miracle – whether it took six days or many centuries.

KING. (*Rising.*) Hm.

> (*He moves as if to disagree with her, then thinks better of it and crosses down right. His impulse is to thank her, but he cannot give her this acknowledgement of her intelligence.*)

You have come to apologize?

ANNA. I am sorry your Majesty, but...

KING. Good! You apologize.

ANNA. Your Majesty, I ...

KING. I accept!

ANNA. Your Majesty, nothing that has been said can alter the fact that, in my country, anyone who makes a promise must...

KING. Silence!

> (*Pursuing his own thoughts.*)

Tell me about President Lingkong of America. Shall Mr. Lingkong be winning this war he is fighting at present? Does he have enough guns and elephants for transporting same?

ANNA. *(Not quite smiling.)* I don't think they have elephants in America, Your Majesty.

KING. No elephants! Then I shall send him some.

> *(Handing her a notebook and pencil from the nearby dais.)*

Write letter to Mr. Lingkong.

ANNA. Now?

KING. Now! When else! Now is always best time.

> *(He sits crosslegged on the floor.)*

ANNA. Very well, Your Majesty.

KING. *(Dictating.)* From Phra Maha Mongut, by the blessing of the highest super agency in the world, of the whole Universe, the King of Siam, Sovereign of all tributary countries, adjacent and around in every direction, etcetera, etcetera, etcetera.

> *(Almost without a break.)*

Do you not have any respect for me?

> **(ANNA** *looks up from her notebook, having no idea what he means.)*

Why do you stand over my head? I cannot stand all the time. And in this country no one's head shall be higher than King's. From now on in presence you shall so conduct yourself like all other subjects.

ANNA. You mean on the floor!

> *(The **KING** nods.)*

I am sorry, Your Majesty. I shall try very hard not to let my head be as high as your Majesty's – but I simply cannot grovel on the floor. I couldn't possibly work that way – or think!

KING. *(He rises and studies her before he speaks.)* You are very difficult woman. But you will observe care that head shall never be higher than mine. If I shall sit, you shall sit. If I shall kneel, you shall kneel, etcetera, etcetera, etcetera.

> *(He makes a hand gesture after each "etcetera", indicating three descending levels.)*

ANNA. *(After a pause.)* Very well, Your Majesty.

KING. Is promise?

ANNA. Is promise.

KING. Good.

> *(The KING sits. ANNA sits beside him, realizes that her head is higher than his and wriggles down until her head is at the same level.)*

To his Royal Presidency of the United States in America, Abra-hom Lingkong, etcetera – you fix up. It has occurred to us –

> *(He stretches out prone, his chin leaning on his hand, his head pointing downstage. Then he notices that ANNA's head is higher than his.)*

It has occurred to us –

> *(He gives ANNA a significant look, and she reluctantly keeps her promise, lying prone, head downstage, so that her head is no higher than his.)*

It has occurred to us that if several pairs of young male elephants were turned loose in forests of America, after a while they would increase –

ANNA. *(Looking up from her dictating.)* Your Majesty – just *male* elephants?

KING. *(Refusing to acknowledge his mistake.)* You put in details!

> *(He rises, and she does also.)*

Tonight my mind is on other matters – very important matters.

ANNA. *(Warmly, knowing he is getting near the subject he really wants to talk about.)* Anything you want to discuss with me?

KING. *(His reaction show he wants to, but he then thinks the better of it.)* Why should I discuss important matters with woman?

ANNA. *(Rebuffed.)* Very well, Your Majesty.

> *(She curtseys.)*

I shall go back to my room. May I say goodnight?

KING. Goodnight!

> *(ANNA goes up toward the terrace, then turns, to give him another chance.)*

ANNA. Your Majesty –

KING. *(Relieved and eager.)* What, what, what?

ANNA. *(To cue him.)* I was wondering. When the boat arrived from Singapore yesterday –

KING. Singapore! Ha!

ANNA. Was there any news from abroad?

KING. News! Yes, there are news! They call me barbarian.

ANNA. Who?

KING. Certain parties who would wish to use this as excuse to steal my country. Suppose, you were Queen Victoria and somebody tell you King of Siam is barbarian. Do you believe?

ANNA. Well, I –

KING. You will! You will! You will! You will believe that I am barbarian – because – there is no one to speak otherwise.

ANNA. But this is a lie!

KING. It is a *false* lie!

ANNA. What have you decided to do about it?

KING. *(After a pause.)* You guess!

ANNA. *(She knows what he's up to.)* Well, if someone were sending a big lie about me to England, I should do my best to send the *truth* to England... Is that what you have decided to do, Your Majesty?

KING. *(Pleased with himself.)* Yes. That is what have decided to do.

   (Suddenly deflated.)

But how?

   (Triumphantly solving his problem.)

You guess *how* I shall do this!

ANNA. Well, my guess would be that when Sir Edward Ramsay arrives here –

KING. Ramsay? Ramsay?

ANNA. The British diplomat.

KING. Ah, yes – on way from Singapore.

   (Angrily misunderstanding her plan.)

When he is here, I shall take opportunity of expressing my opinion of English *thieves* who wish to steal Siam. I shall show him who is barbarian!

   (Noticing her disapproval.)

What is this face you put on?

ANNA. Well, Your Majesty, my guess is that you will not fight with Sir Edward.

KING. I will not?

ANNA. No, Your Majesty. You will entertain him and his party in an especially grand manner. Then they will return to England and report to the Queen that you are not a barbarian.

KING. *(Delighted with the solution.)* Naturally... naturally!

(He paces up and down.)

That is what I shall have intended to do.

ANNA. This is the only way to get the better of the British. Stand up to them. Put your best foot forward.

(The KING, bewildered, holds up his foot and looks at it.)

That is just an expression, Your Majesty. It means... dress up in your best clothes. Show them your most intelligent men, your most beautiful women. Edward admires beautiful women...

KING. *(Suspiciously.)* Edward? You call him this?

ANNA. We are old friends. I knew him in Bombay, before I was married.

KING. *(Considering this.)* Ah!...

(Walking past her thoughtfully, suddenly he turns to her.)

But, shall it be proper for the British dignitary to see my women with no shoes on their feet? Shall it be proper for them to put their best *bare* feet forward? No! Sir Ramsay will go back and tell Queen Victoria I am barbarian. Why do you not think of this?

ANNA. *(Suddenly inspired.)* We shall dress them up, European fashion.

KING. You mean dress them in... dresses?

MUSIC 26: ["SCENE (ANNA AND KING PLANNING PARTY)"]

(Music comes in softly under dialogue as they both start to become excited.)

ANNA. How many women can I have to sew for me?

KING. All women in kingdom. How many dresses?

ANNA. That depends on how many ladies are chosen by Your Majesty.

KING. You shall tell me which of my women are most like Europeans, for dressing like same.

(He crosses quickly to the dais, strikes a gong and shouts:)

Wake up! Wake up, everybody! Wives! Etcetera, etcetera, etcetera!

*(He returns to **ANNA**, who has placed the notebook and pencil on the table.)*

I shall command Chinese artists to paint their faces very pale. And you shall educate them in European custom and manners for presentation.

ANNA. I wonder how much time we shall have.

KING. Sir Ramsay's gunboat last reported off Songkhla. How long he take depend on how many ports he call into. Let us say we have one week.

ANNA. *(Horrified.)* One week! Your Majesty, – one week!

KING. In this time whole *world* was created – *Moses* say! Are there any details I do not think of so far?

ANNA. You must give them a fine dinner – a European dinner.

KING. I was going to.

(In their excitement they begin crossing up and down, scissors fashion.)

ANNA. And a ball. With music.

KING. Music.

(His face lights up.)

And dancing!

ANNA. Yes, Your Majesty. And dancing!

KING. Why do *you* not think of dancing?

ANNA. It's an inspired idea, Your Majesty.

(Now, in answer to the gong, the **WIVES** *enter in nightdress.* **TUPTIM** *is first.* **LADY THIANG** *also enters, but not in nightdress.)*

And we can give them a play. Tuptim has written a version of "Uncle Tom's Cabin".

KING. Ha! We shall give them theatrical performance. We shall show them who is barbarian!

(To the **WIVES.***)*

Line up! Line up!

(Four Amazons enter from up left and divide, two to each side of the doorway. The **WIVES** *form two lines stage left with* **LADY THIANG** *left of center.)*

Lady Thiang! On Saturday next, at nine o'clock post meridian...

*(He turns and looks to **ANNA** to see if he has this correct. She nods.)*

we shall give fine dinner – European dinner. You are to instruct steward during week he shall make eminent European dishes for tasting.

*(**LADY THIANG** bows.)*

I shall taste and schoolteacher shall taste.

*(The **CHILDREN** enter from up right. Still sleepy, they are yawning and, followed by the nurses, form a group upstage right. The **KING** turns to **ANNA**.)*

You say who is most like European lady for dressing like same.

*(**ANNA** crosses to inspect the **WIVES**. The **KING** continues his orders to **LADY THIANG**.)*

You are to make tablecloth of finest white silk for very long table. Also instruct court musicians to learn music of Europe for dancing, etcetera.

(The twins enter and, crossing in front of him, catch his eye.)

What? What? What? Am I to be annoyed by children at this moment?

(A nurse, having lost her charge, comes running after him, clapping her hands.)

Who? Who? Who?

*(All drop to the floor at his angry tone. Then the object of the nurse's solicitude, a **TINY PRINCE**, crawls between the **KING**'s legs and crouches in front of him. The music fades.)*

Mrs. Anna, we must be more scientific with children!

(He walks up and down angrily.)

For the next week, the men and women of my kingdom will work without sleeping till all is ready, and for what is not done, each man and woman shall be beaten a hundred strokes. Everyone must know this, Lady Thiang.

> *(He sees the* **TINY PRINCE,** *still center stage, picks him up in his crouching position and places him, but the wrong way, with the rest of the* **CHILDREN.** *He steps away, realizes his mistake, picks the* **TINY PRINCE** *up once again and places him properly.)*

Tell this to everybody! Above all, I must not be worried by anything...

> *(A loud explosion, a tremendous report, sounding like a cannon, is heard.)*

MUSIC 27: ["FIREWORKS"]

> *(Fireworks appear on the backdrop. Discipline is immediately abandoned, and there are shrieks and cries of fear. The* **CHILDREN** *huddle together with the nurses and Amazons. The* **KING** *and* **ANNA** *move towards the terrace.* **LUN THA** *and* **PHRA ALACK** *enter.)*

ANNA. *(Pointing to the fireworks.)* Look, Your Majesty!

KING. Fireworks!

> *(The* **CHILDREN,** *reassured, move forward a bit to enjoy the show.)*

Fireworks at this hour of the morning! No one may order fireworks but me.

KRALAHOME. *(Rushing in, he kneels before the* KING.*)* Your
Majesty – the British! The gunboat!

KING. They attack?

KRALAHOME. No! They salute, and we answer with
fireworks. It is Sir Edward Ramsay and his party.

ANNA. *(Horrified.)* Now?

KRALAHOME. Now! They must have come direct from
Songkhla. No stops.

ANNA. No stops! Your Majesty...!

KING. Tell them go back! *We are not ready!*

KRALAHOME. Not ready, Your Majesty?

KING. You do not know, you do not know. I had planned
best idea I ever get.

ANNA. Still we do it, Your Majesty – *you* can do it.

> *(The music fades. The* KRALAHOME *rises
> slowly.)*

KING. Ha!

> *(Pacing and thinking aloud.)*

When English arrive we shall put them – to bed.
Tomorrow morning we shall send them on sightseeing
trip.

ANNA. *(Also pacing and thinking aloud.)* We shall start
now, this minute. Work! Work! We have only eighteen
hours, but I shall do it somehow!

> *(The* KING *stops pacing.)*

KING. *(Sternly.) I* shall do it. You shall help me.

ANNA. Yes, Your Majesty.

> *(Resuming his orders, energetically.)*

KING. No one shall sleep tonight or tomorrow. We shall work even when the sun shines in the middle of the day. We shall –

> *(He sees a group of* **PRIESTS** *passing on the terrace.)*

Ah! Priests!

> *(He motions them to come in. The* **PRIESTS** *take positions upstage in a single line.)*

Come, come. Come down. First we shall ask help from Buddha. Bow to him. Bow! Bow! Bow!

> *(All prostrate themselves.)*

> *(To* **ANNA:***)*

Bow!

> *(**ANNA** points to herself as if to ask "Me?" The* **KING** *nods.* **ANNA** *remains standing, but drops her head.)*

MUSIC 28: ["FINALE ACT I"]

> *(As the* **KING** *kneels a tom-tom rhythm begins [vamp in measure 1]. The* **KING** *claps his hands twice. There is a chord of music [measure 2]. He raises his arms, making a semi-circle, palms out.)*

> *(Chanting in meter [measure 2].)*

OH, BUDDHA,
GIVE US THE AID OF YOUR STRENGTH
AND YOUR WISDOM.
AH-H-H-H-H-H ...

> *(In meter and on the beat following his last word everyone [except* **ANNA***] sits up,*

imitating his position and repeating his
chant as the KING *ad libs a free chant on the*
syllable "Ah" [second half of measure 2].)

ALL. *(Repeating chant.)*
OH, BUDDHA,
GIVE US THE AID OF YOUR STRENGTH
AND YOUR WISDOM.

(In meter and on the beat after their last word,
all prostrate themselves. These movements
are repeated for each chant. During the above
the KING *gives* ANNA *a questioning look. Self-*
conciously, she kneels.)

KING. *(He sits back on his heels and claps his hands again.*
A second chord is heard [measure 3].)
AND HELP US TO PROVE
TO THE VISITING ENGLISH
THAT WE ARE EXTRA-ORDINARY
AND REMARKABLE PEOPLE.
AH-H-H-H-H-H ...

ALL. *(Repeating chant as he continues ad libbing freely on*
"Ah".)
AND HELP US TO PROVE
TO THE VISITING ENGLISH
THAT WE ARE EXTRA-ORDINARY
AND REMARKABLE PEOPLE.

(During the repetition, the KING *leans forward*
and down in a crouch, and steals a glance at
ANNA. *He indicates with head motions and*
by the sound of his chant that her head is
higher than his. She accommodates him by
crouching.)

KING. *(He claps one more time, and a third chord is heard*
[measure 4].)

HELP ALSO MRS. ANNA. TO KEEP AWAKE
FOR SCIENTIFIC SEWING OF DRESSES,
EVEN THOUGH SHE BE ONLY A WOMAN
AND A CHRISTIAN,
AND THEREFORE UNWORTHY
OF YOUR INTEREST.
AH-H-H-H-H-H ...

> (**ANNA** *sits up in surprise at the mention of her name and turns to the* **KING** *in protest of his insults.*)

ALL. *(Repeating chant.)*
HELP ALSO MRS. ANNA. TO KEEP AWAKE
FOR SCIENTIFIC SEWING OF DRESSES,
EVEN THOUGH SHE BE ONLY A WOMAN
AND A CHRISTIAN,
AND THEREFORE UNWORTHY
OF YOUR INTEREST.

KING. *(During the repetition of the prayer, speaking to* **ANNA**.*)* A promise is a promise! Your head shall never be higher than mine! A promise!

> (*Reluctantly, she sinks to a kneeling position to match his. There is another quieter chord [measure 5].*)

And Buddha, I promise you I shall give this unworthy woman a house –

> (*The orchestra plays strains of* [**"SOMETHING WONDERFUL"**] *[measure 6].*)

– a house of her own – a brick residence adjoining the Royal Palace, according to agreement, etcetera, etcetera, etcetera.

> (*She moves as if to thank him, but he shushes her.*)

ALL. *(Repeating his words, but as a chant [second half of measure 10].)*
AND BUDDHA,
I PROMISE YOU
I SHALL GIVE THIS UNWORTHY WOMAN
A HOUSE –
A HOUSE OF HER OWN –
A BRICK RESIDENCE ADJOINING THE ROYAL PALACE,
ACCORDING TO AGREEMENT,
ETCETERA, ETCETERA, ETCETERA.

(They remain upright in their prayer positions until the curtain falls.)

(On their first ["ETCETERA"] the **KING,** *watching to make sure that* **ANNA** *imitates him, sits back on his heels. She follows. On their second ["ETCETERA"] the* **KING** *leans forward on his hands.* **ANNA** *follows. On their final ["ETCETERA"] he stretches out, prone. She follows. They are both flat on their faces. Then he raises his head and rests his chin on his hand. She does the same. Fireworks burst through the air beyond the terrace.* **ANNA** *and the* **KING** *regard each other warily. Who is taming whom?)*

The Curtain Falls

End of Act One

ACT II

MUSIC 29: ["ENTR'ACTE"]

MUSIC 30: ["OPENING ACT II"]

(AT RISE: It is the next evening. The schoolroom has been converted into a dressing room for tonight. The floor and tables are littered with dressmaking materials. There is a low bench table right with two bolts of material and a hand mirror on it and another bench table left with a raffia sewing basket and another hand mirror on it. The **WIVES** *are all dressed in their new hoopskirts, mostly finished, but all are uncomfortable in the unaccustomed clothes. Amazons move among them with a tape measure and an ornate jewel box, dispensing and exchanging jewelry. A Chinese artist is painting the face of one* **WIFE**. *Others are receiving last-minute touches from two seamstresses. The faces of the* **WIVES** *are powdered white.* **LADY THIANG** *enters. She has on a western bodice and a penang.)*

LADY THIANG. Ladies! Ladies! Clear everything away! Quickly now!

(The **WIVES** *and seamstresses clear away the materials.)*

ONE OF THE WIVES. Lady Thiang, what is this costume?

(Pointing to penang.)

Here is East –

(Pointing to bodice.)

Here is West!

LADY THIANG. Have too much work to do! Cannot move fast in swollen skirt.

(The music fades out.)

ANOTHER WIFE. Lady Thiang, why must we dress like this for British?

LADY THIANG. Whatever Mrs. Anna wants us to do is wise and good, but this –

(Indicating hoopskirts.)

is a puzzlement.

MUSIC 31: ["WESTERN PEOPLE FUNNY"]

LADY THIANG. *(She sings.)*
TO PROVE WE'RE NOT BARBARIANS
THEY DRESS US UP LIKE SAVAGES!
TO PROVE WE'RE NOT BARBARIANS
WE WEAR A FUNNY SKIRT!
AH-H-H-H-H-H!

WIVES.
TO PROVE WE'RE NOT BARBARIANS
THEY DRESS US UP LIKE SAVAGES!
TO PROVE WE'RE NOT BARBARIANS
WE WEAR A FUNNY SKIRT!

LADY THIANG. *(As she inspects the women's dresses.)*
WESTERN PEOPLE FUNNY,
WESTERN PEOPLE FUNNY,
WESTERN PEOPLE FUNNY,

OF THAT THERE IS NO DOUBT.

THEY FEEL SO SENTIMENTAL
ABOUT THE ORIENTAL.
THEY ALWAYS TRY TO TURN US
INSIDE DOWN AND UPSIDE OUT!

WIVES.

UPSIDE OUT AND INSIDE DOWN!

(A few of the **WIVES** *take off their shoes for* **LADY THIANG** *to inspect while the rest, unaccustomed to wearing shoes, limp about the stage in agony.)*

LADY THIANG.

TO BRUISE AND PINCH OUR LITTLE TOES
OUR FEET ARE CRAMPED IN LEATHER SHOES.
THEY'D BREAK IF WE HAD BRITTLE TOES,
BUT NOW THEY ONLY HURT!
AH-H-H-H-H-H!

WIVES.

TO BRUISE AND PINCH OUR LITTLE TOES
OUR FEET ARE CRAMPED IN LEATHER SHOES.
THEY'D BREAK IF WE HAD BRITTLE TOES,
BUT NOW THEY ONLY HURT!

ALL.

WESTERN PEOPLE FUNNY,
WESTERN PEOPLE FUNNY,
WESTERN PEOPLE FUNNY,
TOO FUNNY TO BE TRUE!

LADY THIANG.

THEY THINK THEY CIVILIZE US
WHENEVER THEY ADVISE US
TO LEARN TO MAKE THE SAME MISTAKE
THAT THEY ARE MAKING TOO!
AH-H-H-H-H-H!

WIVES.
>THEY THINK THEY CIVILIZE US
>WHENEVER THEY ADVISE US
>TO LEARN TO MAKE THE SAME MISTAKE
>THAT THEY ARE MAKING TOO!

ALL.
>THEY MAKE QUITE A FEW!

>>*(The* **WIVES** *resume their last minute preparations as the music continues [pick-up to measure 91].)*

ANNA. *(The music fades out as she enters carrying a stack of folded napkins.)* Lady Thiang, here are the napkins for the dinner. Will you put them on the table?

LADY THIANG. *(Taking them.)* Thank you.

ANNA. Thank *you.*

>>*(***LADY THIANG** *goes out.)*

Now ladies, let me see how you look. Very pretty. Now turn around and get ready for your curtsey.

>>*(The* **WIVES** *spread out and turn so that* **ANNA***, upstage of them, can see their backs. The* **KING** *enters downstage. The* **WIVES** *immediately prostrate themselves, their hoops flying up behing them.* **ANNA** *sees the naked truth.)*

Oh, my goodness gracious!

KING. What shall be trouble now?

ANNA. I forgot! They have practically no –

>>*(Pointing to the upturned hoopskirts.)*

undergarments!

KING. Undergarments?

(He claps his hands, and the **WIVES** *rise.)*

Of what importance are undergarments at this time?

ANNA. *(Stiffly.)* Of great importance, Your Majesty!

KING. Are *you* wearing undergarments?

ANNA. Of course, Your Majesty!

KING. *(Pointing to hoopskirt, derisively.)* That a woman has no legs is useless to pretend. Wherefore, then, swollen skirt?

ANNA. The wide skirt is symbolic. It is the circle within which a female is protected.

KING. Is this necessary? Englishmen are so aggressive? I did not know.

ANNA. *(Going to the seamstresses, who help her remove her smock, revealing a gorgeous ball gown with an off the shoulder bodice.)* I said it was symbolic.

KING. These undergarments – they are devised in symbolic and ornamental manner, yes?

ANNA. Sometimes.

> *(Her gown now revealed, the* **WIVES** *gasp their admiration.)*

KING. Ah!

> *(Looking at her bare shoulders.)*

This is what you are going to wear?

ANNA. Why, yes, Your Majesty. Do you like it?

KING. This is what all the other visiting ladies shall look like?

ANNA. Most of them... I believe.

KING. You are certain it is customary?

> *(Indicating her left shoulder.)*

Etcetera,

>   *(Indicating her right shoulder.)*

etcetera,

>   *(Almost indicating her cleavage.)*

etcetera...

>   *(He quickly puts his hands behind his back.)*

ANNA. Yes, I am certain it is customary. What is so extraordinary about bare shoulders? Why, your own ladies...

KING. Ah, yes. But is different! They do not wear so many coverings up on other parts of body, etcetera, etcetera, and therefore...

ANNA. *(Like any woman who is all dressed up and meets unsuspected criticism.)* Therefore what?

KING. Is different.

ANNA. I'm sorry His Majesty does not approve.

KING. I do not say I do not approve, but I do say...

PHRA ALACK. *(Running on and prostrating himself before the* **KING.***)* Your Majesty, the English. They are in Palace.

>   *(This causes immediate confusion among the* **WIVES** *who huddle in a frightened group.* **PHRA ALACK** *backs off.)*

A WIFE. They will eat us! They will eat us!

ANNA. *(Trying to restore order.)* They will do nothing of the kind!

KING. *(Calling* **ANNA** *to him, he gives her a slip of paper.)* Herewith shall be list of subjects you shall try to bring up for talk. On such subjects I am very brilliant, and will make great impression. You begin with Moses.

ANNA. *(Taking the paper and crowding in some last-minute coaching.)* Now, remember, Your Majesty – Courtwright is the editor of a newspaper in Singapore –

(She is interrupted by the entrance of SIR EDWARD RAMSAY, *who has wandered into the room by mistake. One* WIFE *screams in fright.)*

ANOTHER WIFE. *(Indicating* SIR EDWARD's *monocle.)* Oh, evil eye. Evil eye!

MUSIC 32: ["EXIT OF WIVES"]

(The WIVES, *in an stampede, lift the upstage side of their hoopskirts, hiding their faces, and rush out. From the look of* SIR EDWARD's *face, it is clear that they should have been supplied with undergarments.)*

ANNA. Ladies! Ladies! Come back! Don't – Come back! Oh, dear! Edward! Oh, this is dreadful!

KING. *(Furious.)* Why have you not educated these girls in English custom of *spying glass?*

SIR EDWARD. Oh, my monocle. Was that what frightened them?

(Crossing down to ANNA, *hand extended.)*

Hello, Anna, my dear.

KING. *(Interupting their handshake and startling* SIR EDWARD.) Who? Who? Who?

ANNA. Your Majesty, may I present Sir Edward Ramsay?

SIR EDWARD. *(Bowing, Western style.)* Your Majesty.

KING. I am sorry, sir, my ladies have not given good impression.

SIR EDWARD. On the contrary, Your Majesty, I have never received so good an impression in so short a time. You have most attractive pupils, Anna.

> (*The* KING *is clearly annoyed by the intimacy between* ANNA *and* SIR EDWARD.)

ANNA. Tomorrow you must meet my younger pupils – His Majesty's children. They are making wonderful progress.

SIR EDWARD. I shall be delighted. (*To* KING.) How many children have you, Your Majesty?

KING. Seventy-seven now, but I am not married very long. Next month expecting three more.

SIR EDWARD. No problem at all about finding an heir to the throne, is there?

> (EDWARD *starts to chuckle, but this falls flat with the* KING. SIR EDWARD *then turns to* ANNA, *but it doesn't amuse her either.*)

I – er – I suppose I should apologize for wandering into this room. The rest of the party were ahead of me and...

ANNA. I'm so glad you decided to visit us – to visit His Majesty I mean, of course –

SIR EDWARD. It was your postscript to His Majesty's letter that...

> (*Seeing that* ANNA *is uncomfortable.*)

really brought me here –

KING. (*Suspicious.*) Postscript?

ANNA. His Majesty was most happy when you decided to accept his invitation... Weren't you, Your Majesty?

KING. *(Grudgingly.)* I was... happy.

KRALAHOME. *(Entering, he starts to prostrate himself, but he gets a sign from the* KING *and instead assumes the stance of an English butler.* SIR EDWARD *turns and looks at him in amazement.)* Your Majesty, dinner is about to be served, but – I would first like to present your guests to you in the reception room.

KING. *(Glad for the interuption, he claps his hands happily and goes off.)* Dinner, dinner, dinner!

ANNA. *(To* KRALAHOME, *referring to* SIR EDWARD.) You have met?

KRALAHOME. *(Bowing to* SIR EDWARD.) Your Excellence.

> *(He exits with dignity of a haughty English butler. An off-stage waltz begins.)*

MUSIC 33: ["DANCE OF ANNA AND SIR EDWARD"]

SIR EDWARD. Anna, my dear, you're looking lovelier than ever.

ANNA. Thank you, Edward.

SIR EDWARD. Found a job to do, eh? People you can help, that's it, isn't it? Extraordinary how one gets attached to people who need one.

> *(Listening.)*

Do you hear that? Do you know we danced to that once. Bombay.

> *(She nods.)*

Still dance?

ANNA. Not very often.

SIR EDWARD. You should.

(*He puts his arm around her waist, and they dance.*)

ANNA. Edward, I think we'd better...

SIR EDWARD. Are you sure you don't ever get homesick?

ANNA. No, Edward. I told you, I have nothing there – no one.

(*The* KING *enters and watches them.*)

SIR EDWARD. Anna, do you remember that I once asked you to marry me – before Tom came along?

ANNA. Dear Edward...

KING. (*Interrupting, firmly.*) Dancing – *after* dinner!

(*The music fades out.*)

SIR EDWARD. Oh, sorry, sir. I'm afraid I started talking over old times.

KING. (*Looking sternly at* ANNA.) It was my impression Mrs. Anna would be of help for seating of guests at dinner table, etcetera, etcetera, etcetera.

SIR EDWARD. In that case, we'd better be going in, Anna.

(*He moves toward her, offering his arm.*)

KING. (*Coming between them, offering* his *arm.*) Yes, better be going in... Anna.

(*She takes the* KING's *arm, and they start off left,* SIR EDWARD *following.*)

MUSIC 34: ["EXIT OF ANNA, KING AND SIR EDWARD"]

ANNA. (*After a quick look at the paper the* KING *has given her.*) His Majesty made an interesting observation the

other day – about Moses. It seems he takes issue with
the statement that...

*(They are off. A musical button [measure 9]
ends the scene.)*

Scene Two: The Palace Grounds

(The Palace Grounds. Later that evening.)

MUSIC 35: ["WE KISS IN A SHADOW"] – Incidental

(AT RISE: **TUPTIM** *enters from right, crossing to left center anxiously. Unknown to* **TUPTIM,** **LADY THIANG** *has followed her, and stands center, watching her.* **TUPTIM** *starts to back to center, almost colliding with* **LADY THIANG.***)*

LADY THIANG. Princess Tuptim, dinner is over. King and his English guests are on way to theatre pavillion. Should you not be there to begin your play?

TUPTIM. *(Rattled.)* I came out here to memorize my lines.

LADY THIANG. *(Stopping her as she starts to go.)* I think not, Princess. I have seen you and Lun Tha together. I do not tell King. For *his* sake. I do not wish to hurt him. But your lover will leave Siam tonight.

TUPTIM. Tonight?

LADY THIANG. Now go to the theatre, Princess.

> (**TUPTIM** *exits.* **LADY THIANG** *starts off, stops as she sees* **LUN THA** *enter left [measure 19], looks at him with stern suspicion, then exits.* **LUN THA** *crosses to the other side, and calls off, in a whisper.)*

LUN THA. Tuptim!

TUPTIM. *(Entering.)* Turn back and look the other way.

> *(He does so.)*

I am here in the shadow of the wall. I will stay here until she turns the corner.

(LUN THA watches LADY THIANG off, then turns towards TUPTIM, who runs down to meet him. They are careful. Even when they touch they are aware of the danger they are in.)

She says you will leave Siam tonight, but I do not believe her.

LUN THA. It is true, Tuptim. They have ordered me on to the first ship that leaves for Burma, and it is tonight.

TUPTIM. What will we do?

LUN THA. You are coming with me!

TUPTIM. I!

LUN THA. Secret Police will be at the theatre. Meet me here, after your play. Everything is arranged.

TUPTIM. I cannot believe it.

MUSIC 36: ["I HAVE DREAMED"]

LUN THA. I can. It will be just as I have pictured it a million times.

(He sings.)

I HAVE DREAMED
THAT YOUR ARMS ARE LOVELY,
I HAVE DREAMED
WHAT A JOY YOU'LL BE.

I HAVE DREAMED
EVERY WORD YOU'LL WHISPER
WHEN YOU'RE CLOSE,
CLOSE TO ME.

HOW YOU LOOK
IN THE GLOW OF EVENING –
I HAVE DREAMED
AND ENJOYED THE VIEW.

IN THESE DREAMS I'VE LOVED YOU SO
THAT BY NOW I THINK I KNOW
WHAT IT'S LIKE TO BE LOVED BY YOU –
I WILL LOVE BEING LOVED BY YOU.

TUPTIM.

ALONE AND AWAKE

I'VE LOOKED AT THE STARS,
THE SAME THAT SMILED ON YOU;
AND TIME AND AGAIN
I'VE THOUGHT ALL THE THINGS
THAT YOU WERE THINKING TOO.

I HAVE DREAMED
THAT YOUR ARMS ARE LOVELY,
I HAVE DREAMED
WHAT A JOY YOU'LL BE.

I HAVE DREAMED
EVERY WORD YOU'LL WHISPER
WHEN YOU'RE CLOSE,
CLOSE TO ME.

HOW YOU LOOK
IN THE GLOW OF EVENING –
I HAVE DREAMED
AND ENJOYED THE VIEW.

IN THESE DREAMS I'VE LOVED YOU SO
THAT BY NOW I THINK I KNOW

BOTH.

WHAT IT'S LIKE TO BE LOVED BY YOU –
I WILL LOVE BEING LOVED BY YOU.

(They embrace. **ANNA** *enters.* **TUPTIM** *runs to her.)*

MUSIC 37: ["HELLO, YOUNG LOVERS"] – Reprise

ANNA. Tuptim!

TUPTIM. Mrs. Anna!

ANNA. Tuptim, they are looking for you at the theatre. I guessed you were both here. I ran out to warn you. I do think you're being reckless.

TUPTIM. Yes, I will go.

(She starts away, then turns back and surprises ANNA with a suddenly serious tone in her voice.)

I must say goodbye to you now, Mrs. Anna.

(She kneels, kisses ANNA's hand impulsively, and runs off.)

ANNA. *(To LUN THA.)* Gracious! Anyone would think that she never expected to see me again.

(He looks at her steadily, and catching his look, she crosses in front of him, looking after TUPTIM.)

LUN THA. Mrs. Anna, we are leaving tonight.

ANNA. Leaving? How?

LUN THA. Do not ask me how. It is better if you do not know. We shall never forget you, Mrs. Anna.

(He kisses her hand.)

Never.

ANNA. *(As he goes.)* God bless you both!

(Alone, thoughtfully, she sings.)

I KNOW HOW IT FEELS
TO HAVE WINGS ON YOUR HEELS
AND TO FLY DOWN A STREET IN A TRANCE.
YOU FLY DOWN A STREET

ON THE CHANCE THAT YOU'LL MEET,
AND YOU MEET – NOT REALLY BY CHANCE.

DON'T CRY, YOUNG LOVERS,
WHATEVER YOU DO,
DON'T CRY BECAUSE I'M ALONE.
ALL OF MY MEMORIES
ARE HAPPY TONIGHT,
I'VE HAD A LOVE OF MY OWN.

I'VE HAD A LOVE OF MY OWN,
LIKE YOURS ,
I'VE HAD A LOVE OF MY OWN.

*(She starts off as the theatre pavilion curtain
closes downstage of her.)*

Scene Three: The Theatre Pavilion

MUSIC 38: ["THE SMALL HOUSE OF UNCLE THOMAS (BALLET)"]

(In front of the theatre pavilion curtain [in one], later that evening.)

*(AT RISE: The theatre pavilion curtain opens revealing the entrances of the Royal dancers, dressed in traditional costumes, their faces painted chalk-white. First, a male dancer [the drummer] enters from down right, beating a gong in walking rhythm. He crosses to stage left as other male dancers enter from down left carrying a stand for the gong, a drum, a ratchet and a stool. These are placed far stage left. The drummer, hangs the gong on the gong stand and sits on the stool. As this is happening more male dancers enter from right and place a bench for the singers and a stool for **TUPTIM** far right. At the same time Royal singers (female) enter from left, cross to center, bow ceremoniously, cross to right and take their places, some sitting on and some standing behind the bench. Two of the men are holding the cut out of a small house up center. Two others, behind the background curtain, will part the curtain as the principal characters enter through the house piece. After these entrances the stair unit that will be used by Buddha can be set behind the ballet curtain. **TUPTIM** enters down right, bows and sits on the stool, ready to begin.)*

Scene Four: The Ballet

TUPTIM. *(Speaking straight out at the audience, as if addressing the* **KING** *and his British visitors.)* Your Majesty,

> *(A musical chord.)*

and honorable guests,

> *(Another chord.)*

I beg to put before you "Small House Of Uncle Thomas."

> *(The* **CHORUS,** *whenever speaking or singing in rhythm, beat woodblocks and/or cymbals on the downbeat. This applies throughout the entire ballet. The choreographer should refer to the piano vocal score for all on stage drum, gong, ratchet and tom-tom cues.)*

CHORUS.
SMALL HOUSE OF UNCLE THOMAS.
SMALL HOUSE OF UNCLE THOMAS.
WRITTEN BY A WOMAN,
HARRIET BEECHER STO-WA.

TUPTIM. House is in Kingdom of Kentucky, ruled by most wicked king in all America, Simon of Legree.

> *(Two gongs – On the first gong the dancing corps reacts with a Siamese gesture illustrating fear. On the second gong they relax this pose into an anticipation of Uncle Thomas' entrance.)*

Your Majesty, I beg to put before you loving friends...

> *(On stage drum begins as Uncle Thomas enters.)*

UNCLE THOMAS.

>*(He enters from cabin.)*

CHORUS.
DEAR OLD UNCLE THOMAS.

TUPTIM.
LITTLE EVA.

>*(She enters from cabin.)*

CHORUS.
BLESSED LITTLE EVA.

TUPTIM.
LITTLE TOPSY.

>*(She enters from cabin.)*

CHORUS.
MISCHIEF MAKER, TOPSY.

TUPTIM.
HAPPY PEOPLE.

CHORUS.
VERY HAPPY PEOPLE.

>*(The happy people dance.)*

TUPTIM. *(Measure 53.)*
HAPPY PEOPLE!
HAPPY PEOPLE!

>*(At the end of their dance **TUPTIM** continues.)*

Your Majesty, I beg to put before you one who is not happy— the slave Eliza.

>*(Eliza enters from cabin. Her "baby" is hooked onto her belt.)*

CHORUS.
   POOR ELIZA,
   POOR ELIZA,
   POOR UNFORTUNATE SLAVE.

TUPTIM. *(Chord.)* Eliza's lord and master

King Simon of Legree

   (A loud gong – Eliza reacts in terror. Then a soft gong – Eliza relaxes.)

She hates her lord and master

And fears him.

   (Another gong – Eliza again pantomimes terror.)

This King has sold her lover

To far away province of Oheeo.

   (Mispronunciation of "Ohio".)

   (A chord.)

Lover's name is George.

CHORUS.
   GEORGE.

TUPTIM. Baby in her arms also called George.

CHORUS.
   GEORGE.

TUPTIM. Eliza say she run away, and look for lover George.

CHORUS.
   GEORGE.

TUPTIM. So she bid goodbye to friends,

   (Cymbal.)

and start on her escape.

(There are four triangle beats [measure 72] on which Eliza hops four times towards exit left. This is followed by a forte chord [measure 73] on which she poses. Two more bars of music [measure 74] are followed by a tremelo [measure 76], on which she exits. This is followed immediately by another tremelo [measure 77], on which she reenters.)

The escape.

CHORUS.
>RUN, ELIZA. RUN, ELIZA!
>RUN FROM SIMON.

TUPTIM. Poor Eliza running, And run into a rain storm.

>*(The rainstorm is depicted by dancers waving strips of silk. After the "storm" is over, Eliza shakes the "rain" off herself [Triangle roll] and then her "baby" [Another triangle roll].)*

COMES A MOUNTAIN.

>*(Three male dancers run on and form a "mountain".)*

CHORUS.
>CLIMB, ELIZA.

>*(Eliza climbs the "mountain", reaches the top and descends the opposite side.)*

TUPTIM.
>HIDE, ELIZA!

>*(Dancers holding stylized branches enter and form a "forest".)*

CHORUS.
>HIDE FROM SIMON! HIDE IN FOREST.

1ST GIRL.
> POOR ELIZA!

2ND GIRL.
> POOR ELIZA!

3RD GIRL.
> POOR ELIZA!

4TH GIRL.
> POOR ELIZA.!

5TH GIRL.
> POOR ELIZA!

ALL.
> GIRLS POOR ELIZA!

TUPTIM. *(After last chord of music.)* Eliza very tired.

> *(Eliza poses "tired". Another chord of music as "trees" exit stage right. Music (rachet) continues as Eliza bows and exits.)*

Your Majesty, I regret to put before you King Simon of Legree.

> *(The slaves of Simon run on. Simon, wearing a terrible, three-headed masque, is borne on by his attendants. His slaves prostrate themselves before him in the manner of the subjects of the King of Siam.)*

BECAUSE ONE SLAVE HAS RUN AWAY,
SIMON BEATING EV'RY SLAVE.

> *(Music [measure 149] as Simon dances down the aisle of quivering slaves, slashing at them with his huge sword. A gong sounds. [Measure 157].)*

Simon clever man.

> *(Chord.)*

He decide to hunt Eliza...

>   *(Simon makes a "bow and arrow" hunting gesture.)*

not only with soldiers...

>   *(Simon takes a kneeling soldier position.)*

but...

>   *(Simon holds his finger up.)*

with scientific dogs...

(Simon <u>taps</u> his finger to his temple three times. [<u>SCI</u>-en-<u>TI</u>-fic <u>DOGS</u>].) who sniff... and smell...

>   *(Simon paws the ground with the four fingers of his right hand. Twice he brings them wriggling to his nose, once on "sniff" and once on "smell".)*

and thereby discover all who run from King.

>   *(Simon jumps to his feet.)*

>   *(Music [measure 160] as Simon is lifted by his three attendants and he and his entourage exit up right in three. At measure 174 Eliza enters from right in one.)*

CHORUS.
RUN, ELIZA RUN!
RUN, ELIZA RUN!

>   *(Eliza crosses stage, fleeing and exiting stage left in one.)*

RUN FROM SIMON, RUN!

>   *(At measure 180 dancers with dog masks portraying bloodhounds who "sniff and smell" enter in one from right. They pick up*

Eliza's scent and exit after her. At [measure 191] Eliza reenters in two from left.)

RUN, ELIZA.

RUN, RUN.

RUN FROM SIMON.

RUN, RUN.

POOR ELIZA,

RUN FROM SIMON.

(At [measure 198] Eliza exits right in two. Dogs, now with **SIAMESE GUARDS** *close behind, re-enter left in two and three. At [measure 206] Eliza re-enters from right and crosses the stage a third time, fleeing.)*

ELIZA, RUN!

ELIZA, RUN FROM SIMON,

RUN!

ELIZA, RUN!

TUPTIM.

POOR ELIZA!

CHORUS.

ELIZA, RUN FROM SIMON,

(Shouted.)

RUN!

(At [measure 214] Dogs, Simon, **SIAMESE GUARDS** *and Soldiers re-enter from stage right in hot pursuit.)*

RUN, ELIZA.

RUN FROM SIMON.

(Eliza crosses upstage and across the back and exits stage right in three.)

RUN, ELIZA.

RUN FROM SIMON.

(Simon and his entourage follow in pursuit, exiting stage right in two and three.)

RUN, ELIZA.

RUN, RUN.

(Quasi operatic scream.)

AHHHHH!

(At [measure 223] two dancers [attendants] run on with a long strip of blue silk which they wave to indicate a flowing river.)

TUPTIM.

ELIZA COME TO RIVER,

ELIZA COME TO RIVER.

(Upstage of the "river" Eliza runs back and forth in panic.)

CHORUS.

POOR ELIZA!

TUPTIM.

WHO CAN SAVE HER?

CHORUS.

ONLY BUDDHA,

BUDDHA, BUDDHA, BUDDHA!

SAVE HER BUDDHA,

SAVE HER, BUDDHA, SAVE HER! ...

WHAT WILL BUDDHA DO?

(A gong crashes as Eliza sinks to her knees upstage of the "river", left of center. The background curtains are pulled apart by two attendants. This reveals Buddha [one of the **CHILDREN***] seated at the top of a high ladder in a pose of meditation. To the right of the foot of the ladder stands an angel ["George"].*

The angel holds a golden horn, the kind of horn that identifies The God of Wind.)

TUPTIM. Buddha make a miracle!

(As she speaks, Buddha illustrates **TUPTIM***'s words with a gesture of his hand.)*

Buddha send an angel down.

(As she speaks the angel moves to the "river", which is still undulating wildly.)

Angel make the wind blow cold.

(The angel blows on the "river" through his horn. Gradually it subsides until it no longer ripples. The "river" is frozen!)

Make the river water hard, Hard enough to walk upon.

CHORUS. *(Softly.)* Buddha make a miracle!

(Chord.)

PRAISE TO BUDDAH!

(As they sing the angel moves upstage and hands his horn to an attendant. As the attendants close the background curtain the angel brings Eliza to her feet. They shake hands solemnly.)

TUPTIM. Angel show her how to walk on frozen water.

(Eliza looks down at the river, somewhat puzzled. At [measure 241] The angel places his right foot on the "ice", reassuring Eliza. On [measure 242] she imitates him, placing her right foot on the "ice". He then steps on the "ice" with his left foot [measure 243], and she follows [measure 244]. On [measure 245] he takes both her hands. Their movements

*become a pas-de-deux in the manner of two
skaters. At bar 279 male dancers [three from
the right and three from the left] slowly enter
with long poles like fishing rods, from which
dangle large representations of snowflakes.)*

Now as token of his love,

Buddha make a new miracle.

(As **TUPTIM** *describes this new miracle, the*
CHORUS *continues singing. The "snowflakes"
surround Eliza and the angel, following them
wherever they go.)*

1ST SOLO.
PRAISE TO BUDDHA!

2ND SOLO.
PRAISE TO BUDDHA.

TUPTIM. Send from heaven stars and blossoms.

3RD SOLO.
PRAISE TO BUDDHA.

TUPTIM. Look like lace upon the sky.

ALL CHORUS. *(Building in volume.)*
PRAISE TO BUDDHA,
PRAISE TO BUDDHA,
PRAISE TO BUDDHA.

TUPTIM. *(As she speaks, Eliza and the angel arrive
downstage left.)* So Eliza cross the river, Hidden by this
veil of lace.

*(***TUPTIM** *steps down a few feet. EVERYONE
holds.)*

Forgot to tell you name of miracle: *"Snow."*

(At [measure 299] the Angel and the "snowflakes" exit stage left as Eliza, terrified, looks to see Simon and his entourage approaching from stage right.)

OF A SUDDEN SHE CAN SEE
WICKED SIMON OF LEGREE,
SLIDING CROSS THE RIVER FAST
WITH HIS BLOODHOUNDS AND HIS SLAVES.

(As she intones the above Simon and his slaves enter "skating" grotesquely. Eliza exits, stage left. At bar 310, on the shoulder of a male dancer, the angel ["George"] is brought on holding the "sun". The "river" begins to ripple.)

What has happened to the river?

Buddha has called out the sun!

CHORUS.

BUDDHA HAS CALLED OUT THE SUN!
SUN HAS MADE THE WATER SOFT.
WICKED SIMON AND HIS SLAVES
FALL IN RIVER AND ARE DROWNED.

(As they sing the "river" begins to rise. Simon and his entourage run back and forth frantically, leaping in panic. The angel exits left. As the blue silk "river" rises up and is wrapped around them they are dragged off upstage right and drowned. At [measure 329] a replica of the first cabin, but with snow on the roof and ice on the windowpanes, is brought on in three from the left and is placed diagonally near the third wing.)

TUPTIM. On other side of river is pretty city, Canada, where Eliza sees lovely small house.

GUESS WHO LIVE IN HOUSE?

UNCLE THOMAS.

(Entering from the third wing through the doorway of the new cabin.)

CHORUS.
DEAR OLD UNCLE THOMAS.

TUPTIM.
LITTLE EVA.

(She enters.)

CHORUS.
BLESSED LITTLE EVA.

TUPTIM.
LITTLE TOPSY.

(She enters.)

CHORUS.
MISCHIEF MAKER TOPSY.

TUPTIM.
LOVER GEORGE.

(The angel enters, but this time without wings.)

CHORUS.
FAITHFUL LOVER, GEORGE.

TUPTIM. Who is looking like angel to Eliza.

(Chord.)

They have all escaped from wicked Simon and make happy reunion.

(At [measure 354] the characters do a "Happy Reunion" dance. At [measure 368] the entire ensemble of Royal dancers [without Simon] enters. At [measure 372] they all join in a "Royal Dance of Celebration".)

Topsy glad that Simon die,

Topsy dance for joy.

> *(A chord – Topsy dances a few steps, then strikes a pose.)*

I tell you what Harriet Beecher Stowa say

That Topsy say:

> *(Gong.)*

"I specks I'se de wickedest critter

In de world!"

> *(Another gong. **TUPTIM** frowns, and an earnest, dramatic note comes into her voice. She steps forward, breaking the fourth wall and speaking out front directly to the **KING**.)*

But I do not believe that Topsy is wicked critter. Because I too am glad for death of King. Of any King who pursues a slave who is unhappy and wish to join her lover!

> *(The dancers are frightened. This isn't supposed to be happening. **TUPTIM**'s emotions are running away with her. They look at each other in terror.)*

And Your Majesty, I wish to say to you…

> *(Realizing her dangerous behavior, she recovers.)*

Your Majesty –

> *(A chord.)*

And honorable guests…

> *(Another chord.)*

I will tell you end of story...

(The dancers resume their positions. **TUPTIM** *is back in the make believe tale of "Uncle Thomas." Music continues at measure 387.)*

Is very sad ending. Buddha has saved Eliza. But with the blessings of Buddha also come sacrifice.

(Gong – The background curtains are parted and Buddha is again revealed.)

CHORUS.
POOR LITTLE EVA,
POOR LITTLE EVA,
POOR UNFORTUNATE CHILD!

(Eva comes to center, weeping. **TUPTIM** *continues speaking over the following:)*
POOR LITTLE EVA,

(Eva bows to those on her left.)
POOR LITTLE EVA,

(She bows again to those on her right.)
POOR UNFORTUNATE CHILD!

TUPTIM. Is Buddha's wish that Eva come to him and thank him personally for saving of Eliza and baby. And so she die...

(Eva drops her head to one side and down.)

and go to arms of Buddha.

(Eva turns and reluctantly takes her leave. She begins to climb the ladder to Buddha as the "clouds" are parted by the attendants.)

CHORUS.
PRAISE TO BUDDHA!
PRAISE TO BUDDHA!

(The music mounts in a loud and uplifting crescendo. The theatre pavilion curtain closes on the tragic tableau.)

MUSIC 39: ["POSTLUDE OF BALLET (BOWS)"]

(As the music begins the servants enter stage left and right to clear the musical instruments [left] and the bench and TUPTIM's stool [right]. While this is happening the Royal singers form two lines center [measure 6], bow [measure 9], and exit stage left [measure 15.] Next [at measure 18] Simon and Uncle Thomas [carrying their masks], Eliza, George, Topsy and Eva enter in a line from stage right. All take a formal Siamese pose to the right [measure 22] and then take the same pose to the left [measure 24.] At [measure 26] all bow to the KING and at [measure 28] all except Eliza exit stage left. At [measure 30] TUPTIM, who has remained in place stage right, and Eliza then bow to each other. Eliza exits stage left. At [measure 33] TUPTIM comes forward, bows to the KING and exits stage right. The above entrances and exits will tend to overlap.)

MUSIC 40: ["INCIDENTAL (CHANGE OF SCENE)"]

Scene Five: The King's Library

(Later that evening, after the banquet.)

(AT RISE: **ANNA,** *a shawl around her shoulders, is seated on a pile of books beside the dais. The* **KING** *is walking up and down, distracted.* **SIR EDWARD** *is standing, center, and the* **KRALAHOME** *is in the shadows to his left.)*

SIR EDWARD. The evening was a great success, Your Majesty. I enjoyed Princess Tuptim's play immensely.

KING. This play did not succeed with me. It is immoral for King to drown when pursuing slave who deceive.

(Pacing angrily.)

Immoral! Immoral! Tuptim shall know of my displeasure.

SIR EDWARD. Your conversation at dinner was most amusing.

KING. I was forced to laugh myself. I was so funny.

SIR EDWARD. Her Majesty, Queen Victoria, will be very glad to know that we have come to such felicity of agreement about Siam.

KING. And very happy I am thereof. Very happy.

*(***ANNA,*** *unseen by the* **KING,** *gestures to* **SIR EDWARD** *that it's time for him to go.)*

SIR EDWARD. I think now, with your permission, I should take my leave.

(He bows. The **KING** *extends his hand in a manner clearly showing how unfamiliar he*

is with this Western amenity. **SIR EDWARD**
shakes his hand, then bows to **ANNA.***)*

Goodbye, Anna, my dear. It was lovely to see you again.

ANNA. Goodbye, Edward.

(He goes out, escorted by the **KRALAHOME.**
The **KING** *turns to* **ANNA.***)*

Well, Your Majesty...

KING. It is all over.

ANNA. May I remove my shawl? It is a very hot night.

(She does so. This makes the **KING** *vaguely
uneasy. He closes his own jacket across his
bare chest as if to compensate for* **ANNA***'s lack
of modesty.)*

I am so pleased about everything.

KING. *(Trying not to be too sentimental about this.)* I am
aware of your interest. I wish to say you have been of
great help to me in this endeavor. I wish to make gift.

*(He takes a ring from his finger and holds it
out to her across the dais, not looking at her.)*

I have hope you will accept.

(She takes it slowly and gazes at it.)

Put it on finger!

(Still stunned, she does not move or speak.)

Put it on! Put it on!

*(His voice is gruff and commanding. She
obeys him, slowly putting the ring on the
index finger of her left hand.)*

ANNA. Your Majesty, I do not know what to say!

KING. When one does not know what to say, it is time to be silent!

> (*There is a pause. Both are embarrassed. The* KING *makes small talk.*)

A white elephant has been discovered in forests of Ayuthia.

ANNA. You regard this as a good omen, don't you?

KING. Yes. Everything going well with us.

ANNA. (*Warmly.*) Everything going well with us.

MUSIC 40A: ["GONG CUE"]

> (*A gong sounds off left.*)

KING. Who, who, who?

KRALAHOME. (*Offstage.*) It is I, Your Majesty.

KING. Wait, wait, wait!

> (*He goes to* ANNA *with a vaguely guilty manner and amazes her by replacing her shawl around her shoulders. Then he calls off-stage:*)

Come in! Come in!

KRALAHOME. (*Entering and bowing.*) Your Majesty.

KING. Well, well, well?

KRALAHOME. Secret police are here. They would make report to you.

KING. (*As* ANNA *rises.*) You will wait here.

> (*He goes out.*)

ANNA. (*Deeply concerned.*) Secret police?

KRALAHOME. (*Noticing ring.*) Your finger shines.

ANNA. *(Confused, feeling compromised.)* Yes. The King. I did not know what to say. Women in my country don't accept such gifts from men. Of course, he is the King... Actually it places me in rather an embarrassing position. I was intending to ask him for a rise in salary. And now...

KRALAHOME. And now it will be difficult to ask.

ANNA. Very.

> *(Turns to him.)*

I don't suppose you would speak to him for me – about my rise in salary, I mean.

KRALAHOME. I think I shall do this for you, because this is a strange world in which men and women can be very blind about things nearest to them.

ANNA. Thank you, Your Excellency. I don't understand what you mean, but...

KRALAHOME. No, but that does not matter. And I do not think he will raise your salary anyway.

KING. *(Entering briskly.)* Ha! Good news and bad news come together. You will please stay up all night until we have further report on item of Tuptim.

KRALAHOME. I had intended to do so, Your Majesty. *(He bows and goes out.)*

ANNA. *(Rising.)* Perhaps I had better go too.

KING. No! No! No! I wish to talk with you.

ANNA. Is there something wrong with Tuptim?

KING. I do not know, nor do I consider this the most important thing I must tell you. It is of greater interest that the English think highly of me. Secret police have served coffee after dinner, and listen what they talk, and report conversation to me.

ANNA. You have been spying on your guests?

KING. How else can you find the truth.

>(**ANNA** *shakes her head disapprovingly, but he ignores this.*)

It appears I have made excellent impression. It is clear they do not think me barbarian.

ANNA. This is what you intended to prove.

KING. What "we" intended to prove.

>(*Suddenly switching to the second item.*)

Tuptim.

ANNA. What about her?

KING. She is missing from Palace. You know something of this?

ANNA. (*Frightened, she wraps her shawl more tightly around her shoulders.*) The last time I saw her she was in the theatre pavilion.

KING. That is the last time anyone has seen her. She never speaks to you of running away?

ANNA. (*Evasively.*) I knew she was unhappy.

KING. Why unhappy? She is in Palace of King. What greater honor for young girl than to be in Palace of King?

ANNA. Your Majesty... if Tuptim is caught – shall she be punished?

KING. Naturally. What would you do if you were King like me?

ANNA. I believe I would give her a chance to explain. I think I would try not to be too harsh.

KING. Hmmph.

ANNA. *(Earnestly.)* Your Majesty, of what interest to you is one girl like Tuptim?

> *(She places her shawl up right on the pile of books.)*

She is just another woman, as a bowl of rice is just another bowl of rice, no different from any other bowl of rice.

KING. Now you understand about women!

> *(He picks up a poetry book from the dais and crosses down to center.)*

But British poets... Ha!

> (**ANNA** *crosses right behind the dais and sits on its downstage edge.*)

ANNA. *(Amused.)* You have been reading poetry, Your Majesty?

KING. Out of curiosity over strange idea of love, etcetera, etcetera. I tell you this poetry is nonsense, and a silly complication of a pleasant simplicity.

MUSIC 41: ["SONG OF THE KING"]

> *(He sings.)*

A WOMAN IS A FEMALE WHO IS HUMAN,
DESIGNED FOR PLEASING MAN, THE HUMAN MALE.
A HUMAN MALE IS PLEASED BY MANY WOMEN,
AND ALL THE REST YOU HEAR IS FAIRY TALE.

ANNA.
THEN TELL ME HOW THIS FAIRY TALE BEGAN, SIR.
YOU CANNOT CALL IT JUST A POET'S TRICK.
EXPLAIN TO ME WHY MANY MEN ARE FAITHFUL,
AND TRUE TO ONE WIFE ONLY.

KING. They are *sick!*

ANNA. *(As music continues under.)* But you *do* expect *women* to be faithful.

KING. *Naturally.*

ANNA. Why, naturally?

KING. Because it is natural. It is like old Siamese rhyme:

> *(He sings.)*
>
> A GIRL MUST BE LIKE A BLOSSOM
> WITH HONEY FOR JUST ONE MAN.
> A MAN MUST LIVE LIKE HONEY BEE
> AND GATHER ALL HE CAN.
> TO FLY FROM BLOSSOM TO BLOSSOM
> A HONEY BEE MUST BE FREE,
> BUT BLOSSOM MUST NOT EVER FLY
> FROM BEE TO BEE TO BEE.

ANNA. You consider this *sensible* poetry, Your Majesty?

KING. *(Putting on spectacles, which are set in book.)* Certainly. But listen to this, from your own poet Alf-red Tenny-sone.

> *(He quotes from the book:)*
>
> "Now folds the lily all her sweetness up,
>
> And slips into the bosom of the lake...
>
> So fold thyself my dearest, thou, and slip
>
> Into my bosom..."
>
> *(He looks sternly at **ANNA**.)*
>
> English girls are so – acrobatic?

ANNA. *(Laughing, she crosses to him.)* Your Majesty, I don't know if I can ever make it clear to you... We do not look on women as just human females. They are – Well, take yourself for instance, you are not just a human male.

KING. *(Removing his spectacles.)* I am King.

ANNA. Exactly. So every man is a king and every woman a queen, when they love one another.

KING. *(He crosses down right, placing the book on the downstage right corner of the dais.)* This is sickly idea.

ANNA. It is a beautiful idea, Your Majesty. We are brought up with it of course, and a young girl at her first dance...

KING. Young girl? They dance too? Like I see tonight? In arms of men not their husbands?

ANNA. Why, yes.

KING. I would not permit.

ANNA. *(Easing to the dais.)* It's very exciting when you're young, and you're sitting

> *(She sits on the dais.)*

on a small gilt chair, your eyes cast down, terrified that you'll be a wallflower. Suddenly, you see two black shoes – white waistcoat—a face... it speaks...

MUSIC 42: ["SHALL WE DANCE?"]

> *(She sings.)*

WE'VE JUST BEEN INTRODUCED,
I DO NOT KNOW YOU WELL,
BUT WHEN THE MUSIC STARTED
SOMETHING DREW ME TO YOUR SIDE.

> *(The **KING** eases slowly upstage to the right of the dais, watching her. She rises, easing left.)*

SO MANY MEN AND GIRLS
ARE IN EACH OTHER'S ARMS –
IT MADE ME THINK WE MIGHT BE
SIMILARLY OCCUPIED.

(As **ANNA** *sings The* **KING** *moves to the dais, watching her, a new interest coming into his eyes.)*

SHALL WE DANCE?
ON A BRIGHT CLOUD OF MUSIC
SHALL WE FLY?
SHALL WE DANCE?
SHALL WE THEN SAY "GOODNIGHT"
AND MEAN "GOODBYE"?

(The **KING** *sits on the dais.)*

OR, PERCHANCE,
WHEN THE LAST LITTLE STAR
HAS LEFT THE SKY,

SHALL WE STILL BE TOGETHER
WITH OUR ARMS AROUND EACH OTHER,
AND SHALL YOU BE MY NEW ROMANCE?

ON THE CLEAR UNDERSTANDING
THAT THIS KIND OF THING CAN HAPPEN,
SHALL WE DANCE?
SHALL WE DANCE?
SHALL WE DANCE?

(The music continues. **ANNA,** *carried away by her reminiscent mood, dances around the room until she glides by the* **KING,** *where she stops [measure 62], suddenly embarrassed. The music continues.)*

KING. *(Rising to his feet.)* Why do you stop? You dance pretty. Go on! Go on!

ANNA. Your Majesty, I – I didn't realize I was – after all, in my country a girl would not dance while a man was looking on.

KING. But she will dance with strange man, holding hands, etcetera, etcetera?

ANNA. Yes. Not always a strange man. Sometimes a very good friend.

KING. Good! We dance together. You show me.

(**ANNA** *looks a little uncertain.*)

You teach! You teach! You teach!

ANNA. It's very simple, the polka. It goes

[*Measure 82.*]

(*Spoken in rhythm.*) "one, two, three and one, two, three and, one, two, three and (one)"

(*Singing.*)

SHALL WE DANCE?

KING. (*As he steps left on "One", right on "two", left on "three" and lifts his right knee on "and". Spoken in rhythm.*) One, two, three *and...*

ANNA.

ON A BRIGHT CLOUD OF MUSIC
SHALL WE FLY?

KING. (*Now alternating as he steps right, left, right. Spoken in rhythm.*) One, two, three *and...*

ANNA.

SHALL WE DANCE?

KING. (*Now back to left, right, left. Spoken in rhythm.*) One, two, three *and...*

ANNA.

SHALL WE THEN SAY "GOODNIGHT"
AND MEAN "GOODBYE"?

KING. (*Now right, left, right. Spoken in rhythm.*) One, two, three *and...*

(*He stops dancing and sings:*)

OR PERCHANCE,
WHEN THE LAST LITTLE STAR
HAS LEAVE THE SKY—

> (**ANNA** *points to his feet. He realizes he has
> stopped dancing and begins again.*)

ANNA.

SHALL WE STILL BE TOGETHER,
WITH OUR ARMS AROUND EACH OTHER,
AND SHALL YOU BE MY NEW

ANNA & KING. *(They stop dancing.)*

ROMANCE?

ANNA.

ON THE CLEAR UNDERSTANDING
THAT THIS KIND OF THING CAN HAPPEN,

ANNA & KING.

SHALL WE DANCE?

> *(He offers her his left hand.)*

SHALL WE DANCE?

> *(He offers his right hand.)*

SHALL WE DANCE?

> *(She takes both of his hands as the music and
> her lesson continue.)*

ANNA.

ONE, TWO, THREE *AND*
ONE, TWO, THREE *AND*
ONE, TWO, THREE *AND* ...

KING. *(Joining her, but getting it wrong as he forgets the
fourth count of each measure.)*

ONE, TWO, THREE,
ONE, TWO, THREE,
ONE, TWO, THREE ...

(He stops.)

What is wrong? I know: I forget "and." This time I remember.

ANNA & KING. *(Counting together as they resume dancing.)*

ONE, TWO, THREE *AND*

ONE, TWO, THREE *AND*

ONE, TWO, THREE *AND* ...

ANNA. That's splendid, Your Majesty.

KING. Splendid – one, two and –

(He stops and protests petulantly.)

You have thrown me off count!

(They start again, doing a fairly presentable polka.)

ONE, TWO, THREE *AND*

ONE, TWO, THREE *AND* ...

But this is not right.

ANNA. Yes it is. You were doing...

KING. *[Measure 144.]* No! No! No! Is not right. Not the way I see Europeans dancing tonight.

ANNA. Yes, it was just like that.

KING. *[Measure 154.]* No! Were not holding two hands like this.

ANNA. *(Suddenly realizing what he means.)* Oh... No... as a matter of fact...

(She puts her hands behind her back.)

KING. *[Measure 166.]* Was like this. No?

(Looking very directly into her eyes, he advances on her slowly and puts his right hand on her waist.)

ANNA. (Scarcely able to speak [measure 168].) Yes!

KING. (In the silence [measure 169].) Come!

(On the third and fourth beats of measure 169 ["shall" and "we"] she reaches down and lifts her skirt with her left hand. On the downbeat of [measure 170] they are off. They dance a full refrain and dance it very well indeed, rythmically and with spirit, both obviously enjoying it. At the end they stop for a moment, stand off and laugh at each other. Then he wants more. He advances toward her slowly.)

Come! We do it again.

(They dance again, but only for a few whirls before a gong crashes and the music ends [on "shall we fly?" in measure 209] as the **KRALAHOME** bursts in from stage left.)

KRALAHOME. Your Majesty...

(He prostrates himself. **ANNA** and the **KING** stop and separate quickly, she moving right.)

KING. (Furious.) Why do you burst through my door without waiting?

KRALAHOME. We have found Tuptim.

KING. (A pause. He folds his arms, suddenly stern. His speech is cold and deliberate.) Where is she?

KRALAHOME. Secret police are questioning her.

ANNA. (Terrified for **TUPTIM**.) Now you have found her, what will you do with her?

(*The* **KING** *mounts the dais. The* **KRALAHOME**
rises and moves upstage left of the dais.)

KING. (*Now miles away from her.*) I will do – what is
usually done in such event.

ANNA. What is that?

KING. When it happens you will know.

(**TUPTIM** *dashes on, falls on her knees at*
ANNA's *feet and clings to her skirt. Two*
SIAMESE GUARDS *run on after her and stand*
over her. One is carrying a whip. Two other
SIAMESE GUARDS *enter and take positions at*
the door. **PHRA ALACK** *enters and assumes a*
kneeling position up left near bookcase.)

TUPTIM. Mrs. Anna! Mrs. Anna! Do not let them beat me!
Do not let them!

(*The two* **SIAMESE GUARDS** *drag* **TUPTIM**
away from **ANNA** *downstage center, where*
she remains wimpering. The **SIAMESE**
GUARDS *then take up positions left of center.*
The guard with the whip is level with **ANNA**.
The other guard crouches.)

KRALAHOME. She was found on Chinese sailing ship. See!
She wears disguise of religious student.

KING. (*Shouting down at* **TUPTIM**'s *prostrate, quivering*
figure.) Who gave you this robe? Who? Who? Who?

KRALAHOME. It is believed she was running away with
man who bring her here from Burma.

KING. (*Deep humiliation in his voice.*) Dishonor. Dishonor.
Dishonor.

KRALAHOME. He was not found on boat.

KING. (*Stepping down from dais, to* **TUPTIM**.) Where is this
man?

TUPTIM. I do not know.

KING. You will tell us where we will find him! You will tell us!

TUPTIM. I do not know.

KRALAHOME. It is believed you were lovers with this man.

TUPTIM. I was not lovers with this man.

KING. Dishonor. We will soon have truth of this man. Hoi!

>*(He signals to the* **SIAMESE GUARDS** *and moves upstage. They tear the priest robe off her, leaving her back bare. The guard with the whip raises it, poised to lash her, as...)*

TUPTIM. Mrs. Anna!

ANNA. *(Throwing herself on the guard with the whip.)* Stop that! Do you hear me? Stop it!

>*(Having grabbed the whip arm she throws the guard off balance.)*

KING. *(Coldly to* **ANNA.***)* It would be better if you understand at once that this matter does not concern you.

ANNA. *(Crossing down, she kneels and raises* **TUPTIM.***)* But it does. It does, not only because of her, but even more because of you.

KING. You waste my time.

ANNA. *(Rising.)* She's only a child. She was running away because she was unhappy. Can't you understand that? Your Majesty, I beg of you, don't throw away everything you have done. This girl hurt your vanity. She didn't hurt your heart. You haven't *got* a heart. You've never loved anyone. You never will.

KING. *(Pause. Stung by* **ANNA***'s words, he seeks a way to hurt her in return.)* I show you.

> *(Crossing center, He snatches the whip from
> the guard.)*

Give! Give to me!

> *(He snaps the whip on the floor.)*

ANNA. *(Her eyes filled with horror, she eases up level with
the dais.)* I cannot believe you are going to do this
dreadful thing.

KING. You do not believe, eh? Maybe you will believe when
you hear her screaming as you run down the hall!

> *(Pause.)*

ANNA. I'm not going to run down the hall. I'm going to
stand here and watch you!

KING. Hold this girl.

> *(The two* **SIAMESE GUARDS** *lay* **TUPTIM**
> *face down on the floor, her head pointed
> downstage. Laying down beside her, each
> takes an arm and tenses his feet against her
> body.)*

I do this all myself.

ANNA. You *are* a barbarian!

KING. Down! Down! Down!

> *(The* **SIAMESE GUARDS** *turn their faces away
> from* **TUPTIM** *for self-protection.)*

Am I King, or am I not King? Am I to be cuckold in my
own palace?

> *(He mounts dais and glares at* **ANNA.***)*

Am I to take orders from English schoolteacher?

ANNA. No, not orders...

KING. Silence!

(He hands the whip to the **KRALAHOME.***)*

I am King as I was born to be, and Siam to be governed in my way!

(Tearing off his jacket.)

Not English way, not French way, not Chinese way, *my* way!

(He flings the jacket at **ANNA** *and takes back the whip from the* **KRALAHOME.***)*

Barbarian you say. There is no barbarian worse than a weak King and I am strong King. You hear? Strong.

(He crosses to the left of **TUPTIM** *and raises the whip.* **ANNA** *steps in slightly, watching him. He can not meet her gaze. He runs up center, standing over* **TUPTIM** *and raises the whip a second time. Again,* **ANNA** *moves in close. Their eyes meet and hold. Now, realizing he cannot do this in front of her, he hurls the whip to the left, and in deep shame, runs from the room. After a moment of silence, the* **KRALAHOME** *claps his hands, and the* **SIAMESE GUARDS** *yank* **TUPTIM** *to her feet. They are about to drag her off when* **PHRA ALACK** *crawls forward and speaks to the* **KRALAHOME.***)*

PHRA ALACK. The man – the lover has been found. He is dead.

TUPTIM. Dead! Then I shall join him soon!

(The **SIAMESE GUARDS** *drag her off left, followed by* **PHRA ALACK.** *From offstage we hear a high wailing scream.)*

MUSIC 43: ["MELOS: MY LORD AND MASTER"]

(The **KRALAHOME** *turns and looks at* **ANNA** *scornfully.)*

ANNA. I don't understand you – or your King! I shall never understand him.

KRALAHOME. *(Crossing to her with cold hatred.)* You have destroyed him. You have destroyed King! He cannot be anything that he was before. You have taken all this away from him. You have destroyed him.

(His voice is growing louder.)

You have destroyed King!

(He moves left as if to go. **ANNA**'s *voice stops him.)*

ANNA. The next boat that comes to the port of Bangkok – no matter where it goes, I shall be on it.

(She turns as if to go, sees the ring on her finger, stops, pulls the ring off and holds it out to him.)

Give this back to His Majesty!

(The **KRALAHOME** *crosses to her and grabs the ring. This is the final humiliation for his* **KING** *to suffer.)*

KRALAHOME. *(Shouting, with heartbroken rage.)* I wish you have never come to Siam!

ANNA. So do I!

(She sobs.)

So do I!

(She runs off right. The **KRALAHOME** *stands looking at the ring, then goes off in the direction of the* **KING**'s *exit.)*

Scene Six: The Palace Grounds

(The Palace grounds. Months later.)

MUSIC 44: ["PROCESSIONAL"]

(AT RISE: Townspeople and **CHILDREN** *come on, eagerly watching offstage left for an approaching procession.* **CAPTAIN ORTON** *enters from the left, crossing to center, where he meets the* **INTERPRETER**, *who has entered from right.)*

INTERPRETER. Ah! Captain Orton! Your ship has docked in time! We are welcoming Elephant Prince to Bangkok!

ORTON. White elephant, eh? So that's it. I just passed the young Prince a little while ago. Where's the King? I didn't see him in the procession.

INTERPRETER. *(His face clouding.)* The King is ill. Very ill. He has been ill for many months.

(From off stage we hear four cymbal crashes [measure 8]. On the third crash two female dancers appear from stage left playing cymbals and leading the procession, which crosses from stage left to stage right [measure 9]. Two banner bearers follow, then girls carrying various puppets on poles. They dance across the stage. A dragon weaves on with pairs of human legs propelling it. At measure 41 **CHULALONGKORN** *enters, preceded and followed by Amazons carrying ceremonial umbrellas. Two girls, dressed as exotic birds, accompany the* **PRINCE**, *dancing around him. These are followed by elegantly dressed pairs of ladies in waiting and, finally, pairs of monks, with their arms folded in their sleeves. Before the* **PRINCE** *reaches center*

right, **PHRA ALACK** *runs on from stage left, and bows before him, dropping to one knee and halting the procession [measure 48].)*

PHRA ALACK. *[Measure 49.]* Your Highness! Your Highness! Go no further! Go no further!

CHULALONGKORN. What is this you say?

PHRA ALACK. Your father! Your father is worse!

CHULALONGKORN. Worse!

PHRA ALACK. You are to return to the Palace at once.

CHULALONGKORN. *(Turning to those who are near him.)* Go on with the procession.

*(***CHULALONGKORN*** steps out of the procession, stands as if stunned for a moment, starts to walk off left, then runs off, followed by* **PHRA ALACK.** *The music picks up [measure 58] and the procession begins again, but with all its gay spirit gone. As the procession moves off right the townspeople and* **CHILDREN** *exit nearest left and right. The lights fade.)*

Scene Seven: A Room in Anna's House

(A short while later. The room has been dismantled except for a few pieces of furniture. There is a crate up center and a Victorian chair down right.)

(AT RISE: **LADY THIANG** *is pacing back and forth, looking thoughtful and worried.)*

CHULALONGKORN. *(The music fading as he enters.)* Mother! The Prime Minister told me you where here. I think Mrs. Anna and Louis have already left for the boat.

LADY THIANG. No, Chulalongkorn. Some of their boxes are still here.

> *(She indicates the crate.)*

The servants said they would be back soon.

> *(***CHULALONGKORN*** *walks slowly toward his mother and stands before her.)*

CHULALONGKORN. Mother, what is it with my father?

LADY THIANG. It is his heart.

> *(She sits.)*

Also, for some time now, he does not seem to want to live.

CHULALONGKORN. Mother, I am frightened. I am frightened because I love my father, and also because if he dies, I shall become King, and I do not know how to be.

LADY THIANG. Many men learn this after they become Kings.

CHULALONGKORN. I have been thinking much on the things Mrs. Anna used to tell us in classroom...

>   (*He stops, facing front.*)

of slavery, and I think also on what she has said of religion...

>   (*He looks at* LADY THIANG, *who nods encouragingly.*)

and how it is a good and noble concern that each man find for himself that which is right and that which is wrong.

LADY THIANG. These are good things to remember, my son, and it will be good to remember the one who taught them.

LOUIS. (*Entering, followed by* ANNA. *He sees* CHULALONGKORN *with surprise.*) Chulalongkorn!

>   (*They shake hands.* LOUIS *bows to* LADY THIANG.)

ANNA. Lady Thiang! How nice of you to come to say goodbye. I was down at the ship seeing that all my boxes were on. Captain Orton must sail with the tide.

>   (*They shake hands also.*)

LADY THIANG. Mrs. Anna, I did not come only to say goodbye. I come for one who must see you.

>   (ANNA, *guessing whom she means, turns away.*)

You must come to him. When he heard that you were sailing, he started to write this letter.

>   (*She holds out a scroll she has been carrying.*)

All day he has been writing. It was very difficult for him, madam – very difficult. He has commanded that I bring it to you.

(LADY THIANG puts the scroll into ANNA's hand, then backs up to right of chair. ANNA turns away slightly. CHULALONGKORN steps in.)

CHULALONGKORN. Please read it to all of us.

MUSIC 45: ["SOMETHING WONDERFUL (LETTER READING)"] – Reprise

I would like to hear what my father has said.

(ANNA turns, looks at LADY THIANG, who nods to her, then looks at CHULALONGKORN and moves up to sit on chair. CHULALONGKORN moves in closer and kneels. LOUIS follows him in and stands behind him as soon as ANNA is seated.)

ANNA. *(She breaks the seal on the scroll and reads:)* "While I am lying here, I think perhaps I die. This heart, which you say I have not got, is a matter of concern. It occurs to me that there shall be nothing wrong that men shall die, for all that shall matter about man is that he shall have tried his utmost best. But I do not wish to die without saying this gratitude, etc., etc. I think it is strange that a woman shall have been most earnest help of all. But, Mrs. Anna, you must remember that you have been a very difficult woman, and much more difficult than generality!"

(Tears come into ANNA's voice. She looks up at LADY THIANG.)

I must go to him!

(She starts out.)

Come, Louis!

(They go, followed by LADY THIANG and CHULALONGKORN.)

Scene Eight: A Palace Corridor

MUSIC 46: "[POLKA DOLOROSO (SHALL WE DANCE?)]"

(The Palace corridor. Immediately following.)

(AT RISE: **LADY THIANG** *enters, followed by* **ANNA, CHULALONGKORN** *and* **LOUIS.***)*

LADY THIANG. I will see if he is awake. I will tell him you are here.

> *(She gestures for* **CHULALONGKORN** *to follow her, and they exit right.* **ANNA** *remains left center with* **LOUIS,** *until* **LADY THIANG** *is off, then slowly, followed by* **LOUIS,** *she crosses to right center.)*

LOUIS. Mother, I thought you and the King were very angry with each other.

ANNA. We were, Louis.

LOUIS. Now he's dying – does that make you better friends?

ANNA. I suppose so, Louis. We can't hurt each other anymore.

LOUIS. I didn't know he hurt you.

ANNA. When two people are as different as we are, they are almost bound to hurt each other.

LOUIS. He always frightened me.

ANNA. I wish you had known him better, Louis. You could have been great friends.

> *(Smiling down at him.)*

In some ways he was just as young as you.

LOUIS. Was he as good a King as he could have been?

ANNA. Louis, I don't think any man has ever been as good a King as he could have been... but this one tried. He tried very hard.

  (Pause – **LOUIS** *studies her.)*

LOUIS. You really like him, don't you, Mother?

ANNA. *(Barely controlling her tears.)* Yes, Louis. I like him very much, very much indeed.

  (The music, which has stopped, now continues with the pick-ups to [measure 53]. **ANNA** *and* **LOUIS** *start off as the lights fade.)*

Scene Nine: The King's Library

(Immediately following. A bed has been placed stage left in the KING's *library.)*

(AT RISE: The KING *is propped up on his bed. His eyes are closed.* LADY THIANG *kneels at the foot of the bed.* CHULALONGKORN *is prostrate on the floor at the side of the bed, downstage of the* KING. *The* KRALAHOME *kneels upstage of the bed, never taking his eyes from the* KING's *face. The* WIVES *are kneeling silently in two lines on stage right.* LOUIS *enters [measure 61] from up right, bows formally to the* KING *and backs away right. He is followed by* ANNA *[measure 67], who enters and executes a full curtsey to the* KING. *His eyes open and he addresses her.)*

KING. Many months... Many months I do not see you, Mrs. Anna. And now I die.

ANNA. Oh, no, Your Majesty.

KING. This is not scientific, Mrs. Anna. I know if I die or do not die. You are leaving Siam.

(ANNA *nods.)*

When?

(She sits down on a pile of books at the upstage corner of the foot of the bed.)

ANNA. Very soon, your Majesty. In fact, I can stay only a few minutes more.

KING. You are glad for this?

(ANNA *can find no answer.)*

People of Siam – Royal children, etcetera, are not glad, and are in great affliction of your departure.

ANNA. I shall miss them.

KING. You shall miss them, but you shall be leaving. I too am leaving. But I am not walking onto a boat with my own feet, of my own free will. I am just... leaving.

> *(His eyes close, but he has seen where* ANNA *is sitting.)*

Why is your head above mine?

> *(*ANNA *rises, and* LOUIS *removes one of the books from the pile. As* ANNA *sits again,* LOUIS *stands near her.)*

I am not afraid of that which is happening to me.

> *(He whistles the melody of "Make believe you're brave".* ANNA *looks at him in quick surprise. He smiles and explains:)*

You teach Chulalongkorn.

> *(He touches* CHULALONGKORN*'s head with his left hand.* CHULALONGKORN *brings his head up.)*

Chulalongkorn teach me... "Make believe you brave" is good idea, always.

ANNA. You are brave, Your Majesty. You are very brave.

KING. *(Taking from his finger the ring he has given her once before.)* Here is – something belonging to you.

> *(He holds it out to her.)*

Put it on.

> *(He looks to the* KRALAHOME, *who helps him rise.)*

Put it on! Put it on! Put it on!

(He looks at **ANNA**. *For the first time there is disarmed pleading in his voice and expression.)*

Please wear it always.

(Unable to speak, **ANNA** *takes the ring and puts it on. The* **CHILDREN** *enter, accompanied by the Amazons.* **LADY THIANG** *rises hastily to quiet the* **CHILDREN**. *The* **KING** *hears them.)*

Ah, my children? Tell them to come here.

(The **CHILDREN** *hurry in and prostrate themselves before their father.)*

Good evening, my children.

CHILDREN. *(Together.)* Good evening, my father.

(Then they rush to **ANNA**, *clustering around her, hugging her and greeting her in overlapping speeches.)*

Oh, Mrs. Anna. Do not go. We are happy to see you. We have been unhappy without you. We have missed you so much, Mrs. Anna, will you stay? Do not go away!

LADY THIANG. Hush, children! Did you come to see your father or Mrs. Anna?

KING. *(He has watched the* **CHILDREN** *with interest.)* It is alright, Lady Thiang. It is suitable.

(The children settle on the floor around **ANNA.**)

Was it not said to me that someone had written farewell letter to Mrs. Anna?

LADY THIANG. Princess Ying Yaowlak has composed letter to Mrs. Anna. She cannot write. She only make up words.

(**PRINCESS YING YAOWALAK** *stands up.*)

KING. Speak letter now.

(*The* **CHILDREN** *divide to form a lane through which* **ANNA** *can see* **PRINCESS YING YAOWALAK.** *The princess is uncertain.*)

Say it! Say it! Say it!

(*She turns to the* **KING,** *who nods encouragement to her.*)

YING YAOWLAK. (*Reciting her "letter".*) Dear friend and teacher. My goodness gracious, do not go away! We are in great need of you. We are like one blind. Do not let us fall down in darkness. Continue good and sincere concern for us, and lead us in right road. Your loving pupil, Princess Ying Yaowlak.

(**ANNA** *rises, unable to speak, rushes to the little girl and hugs her.* **LOUIS** *drops down to the foot of the* **KING***'s bed.*)

CHILDREN. (*Clustering around her as they did before, their voices overlapping.*) Do not leave us! We are afraid without you. We are afraid.

KING. Hush, children. When you are afraid, make believe you brave.

(*To* **ANNA.**)

You tell them how you do. You teach them. Let it be last thing you teach.

CHILDREN. (*As* **ANNA** *looks uncertainly at the* **KING,** *their voices again overlap.*) Tell us Mrs. Anna. What to do when afraid? You teach us!

MUSIC 47: ["I WHISTLE A HAPPY TUNE"] – Reprise

ANNA. *(With great effort to control her tears, she sings.)*
WHENEVER I FEEL AFRAID
I HOLD MY HEAD ERECT

> *(The children hold their heads up in imitation of her.)*

AND WHISTLE A HAPPY TUNE,
SO NO ONE WILL SUSPECT
                    I'M AFRAID.
WHILE SHIVERING IN MY SHOES
I STRIKE A CARELESS POSE

> *(Her eyes go to* **LOUIS** *who strikes the "careless pose." All the children imitate him.)*

AND WHISTLE A HAPPY TUNE,
AND NO ONE EVER KNOWS
                    I'M AFRAID.

KING. *(Speaking over the music.)* You see? You make believe you brave, and you whistle. Whistle!

> *(The children look at him, not comprehending. He addresses* **ANNA***.)*

You show them!

> *(***ANNA*** whistles [measure 29]. The* **KING** *motions to the children. They all try to whistle, but cannot. Finally, something like a whistle comes from the twins. This is too much for* **ANNA***. She kneels and throws her arms around them, weeping freely. The sound of a boat whistle is heard off in the distance. Music stops.)*

LOUIS. *(Crossing to* **ANNA** *and tapping her shoulder.)* Mother – It's the boat! It's time!

(The **CHILDREN** *look at her anxiously. She rises and looks at them.)*

CHILDREN. *(Their arms reaching out to her.)* Do not go, Mrs. Anna. Please do not go.

(Suddenly **ANNA** *starts to remove her bonnet and her gloves. She hands them to* **LOUIS** *as she speaks.)*

ANNA. Louis, please go down to the ship and ask Captain Orton to take all our boxes off. And have everything put back into our house.

(A look of relief crosses the **KING***'s face.* **LOUIS** *runs off eagerly. The* **CHILDREN** *break into shouts of joy.)*

KING. Silence!

(At the note of anger in his voice the **CHILDREN, LADY THIANG** *and* **WIVES** *all fall prostrate.)*

Is no reason for doing of this demonstration for schoolteacher realizing her duty for which I pay her exhorbitant monthly salary of twenty... five pounds! ... Further, this is disorganized behavior for bedroom of dying King!

(To **CHULALONGKORN,** *who has remained prostrate below the bed.)*

Chulalongkorn! Rise!

(The boy rises.)

Mrs. Anna, you take notes.

(He hands her a notebook, which has been preset within reach. **ANNA** *sits on the pile of books.)*

You take notes – from – next King.

> (**LADY THIANG** *lifts her head as the* **KING**
> *continues to the momentarily toungue-tied*
> **PRINCE**.)

Well, well, well? Suppose you are King! Is there nothing
you would do?

CHULALONGKORN. *(In a small, frightened voice.)* I ...
would make proclamations.

KING. Yes, yes.

CHULALONGKORN. First, I would proclaim for coming
New Year – Fireworks.

> *(The* **KING** *nods his approval.)*

Also boat races.

KING. Boat races? Why would you have boat races with
New Year celebrations?

CHULALONGKORN. I like boat races.

> *(His confidence is growing. He speaks a little*
> *faster.)*

And, Father, I would make second proclamation.

> *(He swallows hard in preparation for this*
> *one.)*

KING. Well, go on! What is second proclamation? Make
it! Make it!

CHULALONGKORN. Regarding custom of bowing to King
in fashion of lowly toad.

> *(He starts to pace, very like his father, moving*
> *to center.)*

I do not believe this is good thing, causing embarrassing fatigue of body, degrading experience for soul, etctera, etcetera, etcetera...

> *(On the first "etcetera" he gestures right, on the second he gestures left and on the third he crosses his arms defiantly.)*

This is bad thing.

> *(Losing his nerve a little.)*

I believe.

> *(He looks to the* KING, *who turns away.)*

You are angry with me, my Father?

KING. Why do you ask question? If you are King you are King. You do not ask question of sick man –

> *(Glaring at* ANNA.*)*

Nor of woman!

> *(Pointing accusing finger at her.)*

This proclamation against bowing I believe to be your fault!

ANNA. *(Smiling through her tears.)* Oh, I hope so, Your Majesty! I do hope so!

> **MUSIC 48: ["SOMETHING WONDERFUL"] – Finale Ultimo**
>
> *(The music of* ["SOMETHING WONDERFUL"] *begins softly.)*

CHULALONGKORN. *(Clapping his hands twice.)* Up! Rise up!

(A few of the **CHILDREN** *rise. The others raise their heads, but are uncertain whether they should obey him.)*

KING. Up! Up! Up!

(They all rise quickly, **WIVES,** *Amazons and* **CHILDREN.***)*

Two lines, like soldiers.

(They line up diagonally stage right, scaling downstage from the tallest. In the back are the Amazons. In front of them are the **WIVES.** *The boys are in front of the* **WIVES** *and the girls are in front of the boys.* **LADY THIANG** *is down right.)*

It has been said that there shall be no bowing for showing respect of King. It has been said by one who has

(His voice weakening.)

...been trained for Royal Government.

(He indicates **CHULALONGKORN,** *who moves to an elevated position, upstage center. The* **KING***'s head sinks back on the pillow.)*

CHULALONGKORN. *(His voice stronger and more decisive.)* No bowing like toad. No crouching. No crawling. This does not mean, however, that you do not show respect for King.

(The **KING***'s eyes close.)*

You will stand with shoulders, square back, and chin high.

(The **KING***'s left hand drops off the bed. The* **KRALAHOME,** *knowing that he has died, crawls on his kness to the head of the bed, and*

crouches there, heartbroken, and not wishing other people to see that he is crying.)

Like this.

(He stands erect.)

You will bow to me – the gentlemen, in this way, only bending the waist.

(He shows them. ANNA, with pride in her eyes, turns to the KING. She sees he is dead. She moves around the bed to the downstage side and sinks to the floor, taking his hand and sobbing.)

The ladies will make dip as in Europe.

(He tries to show them a curtsey, but cannot.)

Mother –

(LADY THIANG crosses towards the KING [measure 37]. Then with great pride she turns and drops a low curtsey to CHULALONGKORN [measure 41]. As the music swells all the girl CHILDREN and the WOMEN imitate her [measure 43] sinking to the floor as the curtain falls in a final obeisance to the dead KING, a gesture of allegiance to the new one.)

End of Act Two

MUSIC 49: ["BOWS AND EXIT MUSIC"]

(The music for bows and exit consists of one refrain of 9 ["I WHISTLE A HAPPY TUNE"] followed by two refrains of ["SHALL WE DANCE?"].)